BELLES ON THEIR TOES

Belles on their Toes

FRANK B. GILBRETH, JR.

and

ERNESTINE GILBRETH CAREY

Authors of "Cheaper by the Dozen"

ILLUSTRATED BY DONALD McKAY

New York
THOMAS Y. CROWELL COMPANY

Manufactured in the United States of America by the
Kingsport Press, Inc., Kingsport, Tennessee

Designed by Maurice Serle Kaplan

TO MOTHER

who deserves better treatment

FOREWORD

MOTHER is Lillian Moller Gilbreth, and Dad was Frank
Bunker Gilbreth. Their consulting firm of Gilbreth, Inc., spe-
cialized in time saving and in making workers' jobs easier to
do. They were the originators of motion study, and among the
first in the scientific management field.

Dad died in 1924, leaving Mother with eleven children, the
oldest of whom was eighteen. He also left a good many wonderful memories and an "efficiency" system of family life under
which the children helped Mother run the house. Without the
system, without the *esprit de corps* which he had instilled,
Mother's job might have been too much for her.

But it was Mother who made the system work. Mother became the family breadwinner, filled the place of two parents,
guided her children individually through the growing pains of
adolescence, kept the family together. In her spare time, so to
speak, she became one of the foremost management engineers
in the world.

This is a book about the Gilbreth family after Dad died. It
is primarily the story of Mother.

CONTENTS

Contents

BELLES ON THEIR TOES

1

SOMETHING FOR DAD

MOTHER was going to Europe and leave us by ourselves. It was not an easy thing, but it was something she had to do for Dad. For us, too.

Frank carried her suitcases down the front steps to a taxicab parked under the porte-cochere of our house in Montclair, New Jersey. The driver climbed out of his air-cooled Franklin, and gave a hand.

"You the oldest boy?" he asked Frank.

Frank told him he was. Frank was thirteen.

"It's going to be tough on your Mother. All you kids, and you the oldest boy."

Everyone knew it was going to be tough. There wasn't any use talking about that.

"I'll put them on the train myself," said the driver, pointing his head at the suitcases. "I heard about your father."

Frank climbed the stairs and joined the rest of us on the porch, just outside the front door. That was where we usually said good-by when Dad went away on trips.

Dad had died three days before, on June 14, 1924. It seemed longer. He had had a heart attack at the railroad station in Montclair. It had happened in a telephone booth, while he was talking with Mother over the phone.

Dad liked regimentation and for everything to be done by a system. He even had assigned each of us a number, which he used for routing intra-family correspondence and memoranda.

Mother wasn't that way. But from habit we lined up on the porch as we would have for Dad—by ages and in a sort of company front formation.

Anne, the oldest—she was eighteen—was at the tall end of the line. Jane, the youngest—not quite two—was at the short end. In between were Ernestine, Martha, Frank, Bill, Lillian, Fred, Dan, Jack, and Bob.

Anne told us to "dress right" on her. Dad always liked the line to be straight. We waited there for Mother.

We still weren't accustomed to seeing her in black. She looked tense and alone as she pushed open the screen door and came to the head of the steps. We wished she'd let some of us go with her to the boat, or at least to the Montclair station.

Mother stood there, tall, slim, and quite beautiful. Her figure never even whispered that she had had a dozen children.* Her veil was pushed back over her hat, and her face was white and taut.

A few strands of red hair, the only part of Mother's person that wouldn't do her bidding, curled defiantly from under her hat. Everything else was black and white.

Whenever Dad said good-by there on the porch, he always made believe we were secretly glad to get rid of him. Nothing could have been further from the truth, because we worshiped him, and he knew it. But he'd say we were only waiting for

* Mary, the next to oldest, died of diphtheria in 1912.

[2]

him to get out of earshot, before we'd start a wild celebration that would run far into the night. He'd tell us our long faces didn't fool *him* any, and that some day he was going to ride around the block and come back and catch us decking the halls with boughs of holly, building a bonfire, burning him in effigy, and—the biggest sin of all—even using one of his Durham-Duplex razors.

Mother didn't want us to know how she felt about leaving, so she smiled and tried to act like Dad.

"Those long faces don't fool me any," she boomed as heartily as she could. "Just as soon as I'm out of sight . . ." The boom dropped to a whisper, and then she couldn't go on at all. She held out her arms and we broke ranks and burrowed into them.

She didn't trust herself to talk for a while, and neither did we. Finally she pulled herself loose and started down the stairs. Just before she got to the cab, she turned and looked at us—at each one of us.

Mother has a way of making each child know he means something very special to her. Not just as one of the group, but as an individual person who has his own special claim on her heart.

"I love you so," she said quietly. "I wouldn't leave you, if it didn't seem the only way we can stay together later on. You know that, don't you?"

We knew it, all right. Most of Dad's money had gone back into his business. Mother was going to try to operate the business herself—that was one reason the trip to Europe was necessary. If she failed, the family might have to be divided or to move in on Mother's relatives on the West Coast.

Mother's mother had invited all of us to come and live with her, in Oakland, California. Since there were so many of us,

Mother thought it would be a bit of an imposition—more, in fact, than she was willing to impose on anyone, even her own mother. Several of Dad's friends had offered to adopt some of us. None of us wanted that.

"Don't worry about us," Anne assured Mother now. "Everything will be hotsy, honest!"

"I'm sure it will, dear," Mother smiled. "Not only hotsy, but totsy, too."

The driver started to help her into the cab.

"I'm sorry about your husband," he said.

"Thank you very much." Now Mother's voice sounded far away.

"I talked to a fellow that saw it happen. It must have been an awful shock for you."

"Shut up," Frank whispered fiercely. "Why can't he just shut up?"

Anne nudged Frank sharply, and he was quiet.

We got back into line as the cab started down the driveway. We could see Mother waving from the window in the back.

Lillian, who was ten, burst into tears.

"I want to go with Mother," she sobbed. "Tell her to come back."

Anne took two steps and stood in front of Lill, blocking her from view.

"I told you not to do that," Anne said between her teeth. "I told you the first one who did that before Mother left I'm going to murder."

Anne sounded as if she meant it, too.

"I can't help it," Lill cried. "She's got to come back."

All the way up Eagle Rock Way, we could see Mother waving. We smiled and waved back. Lill stopped crying before the car was out of sight, and Anne stepped aside, so that Lill could wave too.

The car disappeared around a curve, and Lill burst into tears again.

"I didn't mean to," she sobbed. "Honest, I didn't."

"It's all right," Anne told her. "We know you didn't."

"Do you think she could see me at the end, when I was waving?"

"I'm sure she could," Anne said. "Of course she could, honey." Anne burst into tears herself.

We went back into the house, and suddenly we didn't feel so depressed any more. Perhaps it was the saying good-by we had dreaded, even more than being without Mother. Mother had gone on trips before, and we had lived through them. And she'd be back in a little more than a month.

"Everybody," said Anne, drying her tears, "did fine. I think Mother was proud of us."

"We'll get things running like clockwork around here," Ernestine told us. "Mother won't know us when she gets back."

We began to see that what seemed the end of everything might really be just a beginning. There was even a certain exhilaration in knowing that Mother had had enough confidence in us to leave us by ourselves.

"Yes, sir," said Anne, almost gaily, "everything went so well that, for the first time, I think we're going to make a go of it." She was fairly beaming now. "Everybody behaved so well I could kiss you all."

"I knew it," said Bill, ducking. "The minute Mother leaves, you start making threats."

Anne grabbed him, and planted a resounding, moist smack on the side of his neck. Bill struggled, giggled, and hollered.

The noise sounded fine after three days of whispers. The tension began to drain out of us.

"I know we're going to be able to stay together," Ernestine said. "I'm so sure of it now that I could almost go build that bonfire Dad always talked about."

"Let's see," Anne grinned. "Where's the nearest holly tree?"

"You keep away from his razors, though," Frank warned. "I'll be needing those one day."

Ernestine and Martha hooted. Bill mentioned something about how the cat would be fully competent to lick off any whiskers that Frank had at present or might produce for years to come. Anne kissed Bill loudly again, and he hollered some more.

Frank ran an exploratory hand across his chin, but there was no sound of sandpaper.

Mother sailed with the tide that morning aboard the *Scythia* for England.

Dad had been scheduled to speak at the London Power Conference, and to preside over a session of the World Congress of Scientific Management, at the Masaryk Academy, in Prague, Czechoslovakia.

Those two honors meant that his work in motion study and the elimination of fatigue in industry were being recognized internationally.

Dad had been a consulting engineer and efficiency expert, specializing in big industry. He was the creator of motion study, which as one skeptic alleged—and Dad never denied—was designed to "make it easy to work hard."

Dad's method was to study a worker's motions, and then to cut down those motions, often by redesigning the machinery that the man operated. Mother was his business partner. She had given him a dozen children and had written with him a half dozen books explaining motion study.

Now she wanted to make certain that he received the recognition the European meetings would bring. And so did we.

She had been invited to substitute for him at the two sessions. At first, it seemed out of the question to accept. And then it seemed to be the one opportunity of keeping the family together. Engineering was, and still is, a man's field. Mother knew there would be difficulties in trying to continue Dad's business. But if she made a success of her two speeches in Europe, before some of the biggest engineers in the world, she might have an easier time in convincing Dad's clients that she could do the work.

Mother wasn't accustomed to making decisions. Those, in the past, had been left to Dad. He had set the pattern, and she had followed it. Even the idea of twelve children had been his originally. But if Dad thought an idea was good, Mother was convinced it was marvelous.

There was a time when Mother wept easily, when she was afraid of walking alone at night, when a lightning storm would send her shuddering into a dark closet.

All that ended the day Dad died. It ended because it *had* to end. It ended because of the realization that what she really feared was that something would separate them.

Well, what she had feared had happened, and tears would not wash out a word of it. So she gave his speech in London and presided for him in Prague. And she was not afraid any more.

AUSTERITY BUDGET

DAD used to complain that if the Bureau of Standards in Washington ever needed a precise definition or an exact measurement of a Jack of All Trades Who Was Master of None, all it would have to do was to build a glass cage, create a vacuum therein, chill to zero degrees centigrade, and send for Tom.

Tom had been with the family for seventeen years as Dad's handy man. The title should not be taken too literally. In a household whose routine was bound by a chain of efficiency, Tom was unquestionably the weakest link.

Tom knew a little something about everything. Not enough to fix it if it were broken, but enough to think he could. He was unwilling to concede that any job was too big for him, or that he had not done a similar, but infinitely more difficult, job before.

He never forgot a mistake, either, and so was able to keep making the same errors over and over again.

Tom was of Irish descent, small, light footed, and tough.

Austerity Budget

Although no longer young even when he first came to work for us, he still clung to the belief that the bigger they came the harder they fell. As a result, he sometimes presented a battered and swollen appearance, and would walk around the house announcing darkly:

"I don't take nothing from nobody, unnerstand? Nothing from nobody."

He was always evasive when asked how he had received the bruises, but would manage to leave the impression that the six club-swinging bullies who sprang on him in the dark, when his back was turned, would be released from the hospital in a fortnight or so.

Tom liked children and animals, and all of us were immensely fond of him. Before Mother left, she had decided it would be necessary to discharge either the cook or Tom, as an economy move. It never occurred to any of us, or to Tom, that he should be the one to go.

"Why Tom," Martha had said, putting into words what all of us were thinking, "would be willing to cut off his right arm for us."

He would have, too. There was no guarantee, though, that in his eagerness to oblige he wouldn't have got rattled and cut off his left arm by mistake.

So the cook had departed and Tom had moved permanently into the kitchen. He now wore a butcher's apron and a chef's cap, and boasted that he never had followed a recipe in his life. This last was all too obvious.

The discharging of the cook was the only economy measure Mother had had time to effect. She hadn't said anything about our cutting other expenses. But Mother made it a policy never to tell us to do the things she thought we were old enough to do without prompting.

[9]

When Mother said good-by, for instance, there was no last minute outpouring about being good, and going to bed early, and brushing our teeth and doing what Anne told us.

We knew Mother wanted those things done, so there was no need for her to repeat them. She may have worried—of course she worried—about whether we'd do them or not. But she didn't intend to show any lack of confidence unless we gave her reason.

There was no doubt that the immediate problem was saving money. For the time being, perhaps indefinitely, there would be little or no money coming in. When there are eleven children in a family, there is always money going out.

We talked economy in the dining room before lunch, an hour or so after Mother's departure. From an odor not unlike that of burning leaves, we gathered that Tom was having trouble with the cooking again. Part of the economy drive would have to be aimed in that direction.

Anne had been left $600 to run the family during Mother's five-week absence. That included the cost of our tickets to Nantucket, Massachusetts, because we intended to spend the summer at our cottage there, as usual. Mother had made the boat reservations to Nantucket, an island off Cape Cod, and Anne was to pay for them when we picked them up.

We thought it would be a good idea to spend only $300, and to turn the rest back to Mother, as a surprise, when she joined us at Nantucket.

"In the first place," Anne told us, "there is the milk bill. Thirteen quarts a day. More than three gallons."

Anne was sitting at Mother's place, at the head of the oval dining-room table. As the oldest one at home, the senior officer present, she was automatically in command. Ten feet away, in Dad's place, sat Frank. The rest of us, including Bob and

Jane, who were still in high chairs, sat around the perimeter.

Anne had Dad's check stubs, some bills, and the family budget book spread out before her.

"The milk bill alone amounts to more than $50 a month," she said. "I don't see how Daddy paid for all these things. Cheaper by the dozen, nothing!"

We decided we could get along with only nine quarts, without anyone dying of malnutrition.

"Each of us is going to have to sacrifice a little," Anne continued, thumbing through the check stubs.

She called out the amounts on the stubs and what they were for. Food and clothes. We were going to have to cut down on them. Doctors' bills. We didn't intend to have any. Dentists' bills. Everybody's teeth that needed straightening had been straightened. Tobacco. Certainly not. Gasoline. We had already sold Dad's car. Dancing school. . . .

"Frank and I," Bill suggested, "could do our part by cutting out dancing school." Bill was eleven, and it was a fight every Monday afternoon to get him into his Buster Brown collar and patent-leather pumps.

"We *couldn't* ask you to do that," Martha smirked.

"We're willing to sacrifice a little," Bill said.

Dancing school went into the discard, and Bill ran a relieved finger around his soft and unbuttoned collar. Also abandoned were music lessons, which everybody sacrificed without too much reluctance. We drew the line at cutting allowances, since all of us thought Dad kept them trimmed pretty close to the bone. But we did institute a series of fines that would reduce our take-home pay. Leaving on an electric light or the cold water would cost the offender two cents; hot water, four cents; failure to do any of the things on the process charts, five cents.

Dad had the household organized on an efficiency basis,

just as he organized a factory. He believed that what worked in a household would work in a factory, and what worked in a factory would work in a household—especially if the household happened to have eleven children.

The process charts, first developed for industry, were an example. They told each of us what we were supposed to do, and when we were supposed to do it.

The charts were in the boys' and girls' bathrooms, upstairs. They listed duties such as washing the dishes, making the beds, combing hair, brushing teeth, weighing ourselves, listening for fifteen minutes a day to French and German language records on the phonograph, sweeping, and dusting.

Dad had things broken down to such a fine point that Lillian, who wasn't tall enough to reach table tops and high shelves, dusted the legs and the lower shelves. Ernestine did the tops and the high shelves.

We decided we could eat much more cheaply if we cut out roasts and steaks, except perhaps on Sundays. Ernestine was a good shopper, so she would plan the meals, stressing such items as frankfurters and baked beans, and she would do most of the buying. We already got our canned goods from wholesalers, so we couldn't save there.

Ernestine also would try to teach Tom the necessity for putting such ingredients as baking powder into the corn muffins, and of adding water to fresh vegetables before placing them on the stove.

Martha, who was the most efficient of all of us and could keep her money the longest, was put in charge of the budget. She also would supervise the packing of clothes for Nantucket.

We talked about the matter of college. Anne had just completed her sophomore year at Smith. Dad wasn't a college man himself, but had believed that two colleges were better than

Austerity Budget

one. At Dad's suggestion, Anne had made plans to transfer that fall to the University of Michigan.

Ernestine had graduated from high school the night before Dad died. She was registered at Smith and was to start taking her college board examinations in a couple of days.

We knew Mother wouldn't allow either of the girls to change plans. She insisted that somehow or other she was going to send all of us through college. Dad had wanted that.

As for our getting odd jobs to contribute to the income, maybe that would come later. For the time being, at least for the summer, all the older ones would be needed at home.

"I don't have to tell you," Anne said, looking significantly at the bigger children, "that a lot depends on how things go this summer."

"I wouldn't want anyone to adopt me, would you Dan?" Fred asked. Fred was seven and he and Dan, who was one year younger, were inseparable.

"Heck, no," said Dan. "I wouldn't *let* anyone adopt me, would you, Fred?"

"Where did you ever get an idea like that?" Anne asked. "Nobody's going to be adopted, especially if everything goes smoothly while Mother's gone."

By the time that Tom announced lunch was ready, all of the duties had been allocated and the new economy budget was in balance.

It was Ernestine's turn to bring in the food. She eyed askance a leg of lamb that she carried in from the kitchen. It was burned almost black and was festooned with charred tomato halves, which looked as if they had become a part of the lamb—a part that needed lancing and bandages.

Ernestine was the only member of the family who didn't get along well with Tom. They had had a running feud that had started years before, when she had proudly presented him a picture of herself and he had announced that he intended to hang it in the pantry as a rat repellent.

Now, without saying anything, but with the face of a martyr who intended to cooperate if it meant poisoning all of us, Ernestine placed the platter in front of Anne.

Anne was caught off guard. "What," she shouted in genuine alarm, "is that? Get it out of here quickly, you hear me? And tell Tom no one is in the mood for his jokes."

"It is supposed to be a leg of lamb," Ernestine said through pursed lips.

"How do you know?" Anne challenged distrustfully.

"I asked him and that's what he said. Leg of lamb."

Anne turned the platter around, studying the contents from all angles. "Any lamb with a leg like that," she said, "had better see a veterinarian."

"I'm beginning to think we should have kept the cook and got rid of that man," Ernestine announced.

"Hush!" Anne warned. "He'll hear you."

"I don't care if he does."

Tom appeared red faced and furious at the butler's-pantry door.

"You don't, eh," he shouted, reaching behind him to untie his apron. "All right, just for that I quit."

Tom sometimes quit as often as three times in a single day, so the dramatic announcement didn't have too much effect.

"I don't have to work here, you know," he continued. "I ain't no slave." He took off the apron and waved it in Ernestine's face.

"No one wants you to quit," Anne told him. "We all know

[14]

we couldn't get along without Tom, don't we Ernestine?"

Ernestine caught Anne's threatening glance and finally nodded reluctantly. "I suppose so," she said.

"There," Anne smiled sweetly. "You see?"

"What's the matter with the lamb?" Tom asked, somewhat mollified.

"Nothing," Anne replied, "except that it seems just a mite well done. We like our lamb just a little rarer."

"It's lamb rangoon," said Tom, as if that clinched the argument. "And lamb rangoon has to be well done."

"Well why didn't you say so?" Anne asked. "That explains everything."

"Nobody never gives me a chance to explain nothing around here, that's why," Tom mumbled, as he disappeared into the kitchen, tying his apron back on. "You work and slave to make them a special dish like lamb rangoon and then they try to fire you. After seventeen years with the family, too."

"It still looks like something that had better not be touched until the coroner arrives," Ernestine whispered.

"Lamb rangoon," Anne muttered. "I've seen rubber boots that looked more appetizing." Then, realizing that as the oldest she was setting a bad example, she started carving, and added: "I'll bet it's good, though."

"Yummy," said Martha sarcastically.

"We'll try to get the cooking straightened out before Mother comes back," Anne promised. "Come on, now. Get the rest of the food, Ernestine. And bring in some cold cereal, will you, for those who don't want lamb."

Bill developed a high fever and broke out with spots that afternoon. By the time the doctor arrived, Ernestine and Martha were feverish and pimply. Ernestine wanted to cover herself with cold cream and powder, and still take her examinations, but the doctor put her to bed. By noon the next day, all eleven of us were broken out and bedridden.

TROUBLED WATERS, AND OIL

No CATASTROPHE ever befell any of us but that Tom, sometime in the distant past, had experienced the same trouble, only more so.

If one of our boys stepped on a nail, Tom would allay fears of lockjaw by describing how *he* once had stepped on a *spike* that went all the way through his foot and into his ankle. Not only that, but he'd take off his shoe and show you the scar.

When Bill broke out with spots, Tom was the first to discover them and hurriedly ordered Bill to bed.

"But I don't feel sick," Bill protested. "Just scratchy."

"Don't tell me nothing," Tom commanded. "You're sick as a dog."

"Just scratchy," Bill repeated, scratching himself.

"I tole you oncst, and I ain't going to tell you again," Tom said. "Get to bed, now. And if you don't stop scratching yourself you'll be out of the Club for a hundret years."

Only members of Tom's Club were admitted to the kitchen after supper. This was true even before he became cook, because Tom always had presided over the kitchen once the day's duties were done.

For Club members who were in good standing, Tom sometimes would play the harmonica, pop corn, distribute candy, and perform card tricks. Those who were out of the Club could come no closer to the activities than the back hall. The door was left open, and they were allowed to watch, but not to eat or otherwise participate.

The older children, while professing scorn for Tom's Club, frequently were found in the kitchen after supper—if they were fortunate enough to be in his good graces. To the younger ones, banishment from the Club was Siberia's steppes.

Tom's minimum excommunication, when meting out expulsion, was for a hundred years. Actually, this meant only about fifteen minutes, because Tom's heart was soft. The maximum, anathema, was for a thousand years and four days. This might mean an entire evening, although the sentence was often mitigated if one could manage to look repentant enough.

After Bill had climbed into his pajamas, Tom called Anne to break the news.

"Oh, Lord," Anne groaned. "That's the last straw! Just when I was beginning to think things might go smoothly."

"It's all right, Anne," Bill assured her. "I don't feel sick."

"I hear you scratching under them covers," Tom warned him. "I ain't deef, you know. I ain't blind. I tole you twicst, and I ain't going to tell you again. Mind now!"

"I better call the doctor," Anne sighed.

"I could tell you how to dose him," Tom said, "but . . ."

"Oh, no you don't," Bill shouted. "I know your doses."

"Remember what Dad told you about dosing them," Anne said.

"I remember." Tom's tone was injured. "I could cure Bill, but I got my orders. I can take a hint."

Anne leaned over and studied Bill's spots. "It looks like a rash or the hives to me," she said.

"Hives," Tom grunted. "He's sick as a dog, I tell you. Of course, he ain't as sick as I was oncst when . . ."

"He ate some of that burned rangoon—" Anne stopped quickly. "Maybe he ate something that didn't agree with him."

"Didn't agree with him?" Tom asked. And then accusingly to Bill: "Have you been sneaking out and eating down street again? You don't know what goes into the food they give you at them drug stores."

Bill shook his head.

"Anyway, it ain't his stomach," said Tom. "I know what it is, all right, but your father give me my orders, so I dassent tell you."

"He gave them to you the time we had the measles and you said it was scarlet fever, didn't he Tom?" Bill said.

"That was the time," Tom conceded.

"Heck, anyone can make a mistake like that, eh Tom?" Bill asked. Bill was one of Tom's defenders, and usually in the Club.

"You scared Mother half to death," Anne said accusingly.

"I still ain't sure it *wasn't* that, neither," said Tom.

Anne went to telephone Dr. Burton, and Tom paced the floor of the room shared by Frank and Bill.

"Of course," he muttered for the benefit of those of us who had assembled to see Bill's spots, "I don't know nothing about it. I'm stupit, I am. I'm so stupit that even though I seen a hundret cases just like it in the war, I don't know what it is. I seen them dying like flies from it."

"Is it really bad?" Bill asked. "Will everybody catch it?"

"You'll catch it, you bold thing you, if you don't stop scratching. You'll be out of the Club for a hundred years."

"Not that!" Ernestine protested in mock terror. "Anything but that."

Tom pretended not to hear. But there was no doubt that Ernestine—or the Princess, as Tom sometimes called her with an exaggerated courtesy—was out of the Club for a thousand years and four days.

Tom resumed his pacing and mumbling. "I was an orderly in a horsepittle for ten months during the war for nothing. Had my eyes closed all the time. Sure I did."

The war to which Tom alluded was the Spanish-American. If, as Tom frequently alleged, he actually had served as a hospital orderly, medicine had progressed considerably since those days. For Tom placed all of his reliance on quinine and castor oil. And we weren't completely sure he knew that the practice of bleeding the patient had been pretty generally discontinued.

What was good medicine for humans, he believed, was equally beneficial for animals. Tom was a collector of pets, both wild and domesticated, much to the disgust of Dad. Dad used to complain that feeding almost a score of human mouths was more than any white man's burden, and that it was an outrage to be required to give sustenance to the fauna which followed Tom home or begged handouts on the kitchen window sill.

Let one of Tom's pets show up with a warm nose, sagging beak, coated tongue, fetid breath, or bloodshot eye, and Tom would swiftly mix a dose of castor oil and Quinine Remedy, add a bit of sugar to make the dose more palatable, and force the solution through the mouth or down the bill of the debilitated creature.

None of them ever died or seemed to hold a lasting grudge. But Tom's cat, Fourteen—Tom numbered his cats progressively —would get down on her belly and start sneaking toward the back door every time she saw him reach up over the kitchen sink, where he kept the Quinine Remedy.

Tom's diagnoses for persons other than himself were varied, uninhibited, and sometimes exotic. But when he was sick himself, he always diagnosed the ailment as pleurisy, regardless of whether the symptoms were a bleeding nose or a swollen foot. On these occasions, he would send out for the Quinine Remedy's large economy flagon, and it never failed him.

Ernestine and Martha were in bed too by the time Dr. Burton arrived. Whenever the doctor came to our house, Tom was the medical orderly again. He said "Yes, sir," and "No, sir," and he sucked in his stomach. Dr. Burton knew of Tom's claims of medical experience, and assured himself of Tom's cooperation by treating him as a learned colleague in the profession.

"What is it?" Anne asked anxiously, as Dr. Burton leaned over Bill's bed. "Tom keeps hinting that it's something serious."

"He says he's seen them die like flies from it," Bill said. "But all it does is itch."

"It's obvious, eh Tom?" said the physician.

"Yes, sir. Only I wouldn't tell them nothing because Mr. Gilbreth made me promise."

"Anyone can see it's chicken pox. No need to make an examination, would you say so, Tom?"

"Is that all," Anne sighed.

"That's what I thought, sir," said Tom. "Either that or smallpox, I wasn't sure which."

"It's nothing to worry about," Dr. Burton told Anne.

"I'm not worried," said Anne, glaring at Tom, "now that I know it isn't leprosy or cholera."

"You'll all be up and around again in a few days," Dr. Burton assured her.

"What do you mean, 'all'?" Anne asked. "Chicken pox is a children's disease, isn't it?"

"Have any of you had chicken pox?"

"I guess not," Anne admitted.

"Then you'll all get it. But Tom will take good care of you."

"Yes, *sir*," Tom beamed.

"I'll have some medicine sent around," the doctor continued. "And Tom, I'll count on you to see they keep regular."

"I've got just the thing," said Tom, and it was obvious that Dr. Burton's medical standing had skyrocketed in his estimation.

"Castor oil," moaned Bill.

"A little castor oil never hurt anyone," Dr. Burton agreed.

"Did you hear that, Tom?" Bill said, grasping at a straw. "Dr. Burton says a little."

"That's right," the doctor cautioned. "Not too much." He turned to Tom. "I suppose you've had chicken pox?"

"No, sir," said Tom. "When I was a kid I had something that looked just like it. Some people even *said* it was chicken pox. But it turned out to be . . ."

"Pleurisy," Dr. Burton nodded sagely.

"That's the only disease that ever give me any trouble."

The next day, when it became apparent that all of us had chicken pox, Anne had Tom move all the boys' beds into Frank's and Bill's room, and all the girls' beds into Mother's and Dad's room. The rooms were adjacent, and by leaving the door open Anne could supervise both wards from her bed.

Troubled Waters, and Oil

Anne had no intention of letting any mass epidemic interfere with the family routine. She had each of us get up long enough to wash, remake our beds, weigh ourselves, and make the notations on the process charts.

We got the phonograph from the boys' bathroom—we usually listened to the language records while we were taking baths or otherwise occupied in what Dad called periods of unavoidable delay—and set it up in the doorway between the two wards. We played French and German records for fifteen minutes. Then Anne got up and looked at the charts, to make sure everyone had done what he was supposed to do.

"That's fine," she sighed as she crawled back into bed. "Now we can enjoy poor health. And a pox on the first person who gets me up again."

None of us felt very sick. We sang for a while, with the boys' ward carrying the melody and the girls' ward an alto. Sometimes, to get the song just right, the boys would sing their part alone, and the girls would sing theirs alone, and then we'd try them together. We sang "Yes, We Have No Bananas," "Oh, Gee, Oh, Gosh, Oh, Golly, I'm in Love," "Last Night on the Back Porch," "You've Got to See Mama Every Night or You Can't See Mama at All."

Then we played some of the new dance records and sang along with them. "What'll I Do?" "All Alone by the Telephone," "Charlie My Boy," "Limehouse Blues," and "The Prisoner's Song."

We didn't mind being sick, and we hoped Mother wouldn't find out and worry about us.

After a while we could hear the sound of a spoon clinking against a glass down in the kitchen, and we knew Tom was mixing castor oil with orange juice and sugar. All of the boys, from Frank on down the line, immediately feigned deep sleep.

Tom brought the castor oil upstairs, one glass at a time. The stirring grew progressively louder as he mounted the back stairs and walked through the upstairs hall to the wards.

When he arrived with the first dose, the boys were snoring. "You don't fool me none," Tom told them. "I can see them eyes winking. I'll be up with your medicine in a few minutes."

He knocked noisily on the open door of the girls' ward, with his head modestly averted. Tom always made an elaborate ceremony of knocking before entering one of the girls' rooms. He thought that the knocking was a waste of time, and alleged that he had, at one time or another, changed all of their diapers. But Dad and Mother insisted on it. When Tom did, by mistake, happen on one of the girls who was not fully dressed, he never could understand—or made believe he couldn't understand—the ensuing commotion. "That's all right," he'd say, while the girl dived shrieking into a closet. "It don't embarrass me none. I don't mind. I don't mind."

Now, after knocking, he asked:

"All right if I come in, Anne?" He stirred the castor oil harder and louder than ever.

"I guess so," Anne conceded.

"Ain't nobody here," said Ernestine, "but us chicken poxers."

Tom entered and bowed low to Ernestine, the Princess.

"Here you are, Your Highness," he said. "I've brung you a present from the Grand Doochess."

He held out the glass.

"Anne first," Ernestine protested. "She's the oldest. Besides, you've probably spiked my drink."

"Where'd you learn talk like that?" said Tom, genuinely shocked. "I'm going to tell your Mother on you when she gets home."

Troubled Waters, and Oil

"Here, hand me that glass and for goodness' sake be quiet, both of you," said Anne.

"Oh, what's the use," Ernestine wailed. "All right, give it to me."

Having reached the decision, she grabbed the glass before her will power deserted her, and drained it.

"Good girl, Ernie," Tom beamed. "You're in the Club. How was it?"

Remembering she was supposed to set a good example, she smiled bravely.

"Delicious," she gulped. "Positively delicious."

"See what I tole you?" Tom said. "The orange juice cuts the taste."

"That's right," Ernestine lied. "Positively delicious."

"Do you want some more?" Tom asked hopefully. "I wouldn't mind fixing you another glass."

"No," Ernestine shouted. "I mean, no thank you. It was mighty good, but that was plenty."

"Tomorrow, then," said Tom, as he departed for the kitchen to mix Anne's dose.

"I never had so much castor oil in my life," Ernestine whispered to Anne. "The old idiot must think I'm as irregular as a French verb."

"If you don't mind," Anne pleaded, "please keep quiet until I've had mine. My heart bleeds for you, but please hold your oily tongue."

Anne, Martha, and finally Frank all faced up to their responsibilities by taking their medicine and managing to smack their lips and say it was good. But when Tom came to Bill the era of cooperation ended.

In the first place, Bill wouldn't wake up, and the more Tom shook him, the louder he snored.

[25]

"I never seen such a sound sleeper," said Tom, deciding it was time for psychology. "Well, if I can't wake him for his castor oil, I'd better do the next best thing."

Bill's snores shook the bedroom.

"Does anyone," said Tom, "know where the hot water bag is?"

Bill thought he knew what that meant. He rolled over and opened an eye.

"Where am I?" he asked sleepily. "What time is it?"

"It's time," said Tom, shoving a glass in Bill's face, "to drink this."

"What is it?" Bill asked, stalling as long as possible.

"You know what it is," hollered Tom, whose patience was becoming exhausted. "Now swalley it."

"I don't like it."

"How do you know you don't like it, when you ain't tasted it?"

"I've tasted it before. It tastes nasty."

"Look," Tom said deliberately. "Ast Anne. Ast Ernestine. Ast Martha. Ast Frank. It's good. It's delicious."

"I know them. They're just setting good examples."

Tom now played his hole card.

"Look," he purred, "I've got another glass just like this one, out in the hall. If you be a good boy and drink this, I'll drink that—just to show you how good it is."

By now all of the younger boys were frankly awake, and watching. Bill considered the offer carefully.

"How do I know," he asked suspiciously, "that there's castor oil in the other glass?"

"You can take my word for it, can't you?" Tom was shouting again.

"I don't think so."

[26]

"Call me a liar, then," said Tom. "Call me a liar."

He went to the hall and came back holding a glass in each hand.

"Take your choice. If that ain't fair, I don't know what is."

"When I take mine, will you drink a glass with me?" Fred asked.

"Sure," said Tom. "It's delicious. Ast Anne."

"How about me?" Dan wanted to know.

"Certainly."

"And me?" said Jack.

"Me, too," Lillian shouted from the girls' ward.

"Everybody," Tom agreed. "All hands and the cook."

Bill examined the glasses closely, and the girls came in to watch him make his choice. The glasses contained the same amount of orange juice, but there was one very obvious difference. On the surface of the juice in one glass were only a few bubbles of oil. On the surface of the other floated almost a half-inch of solid oil.

"I'll take this one," said Bill, pointing to the glass with a few bubbles.

"You're sure you want that one?" Tom asked innocently. "I don't see no difference."

"Don't try to wiggle out of it," said Bill. "That's the one I want."

He was about to take the glass, when he looked up and saw Ernestine just barely shake her head.

"Sure you don't want to change your mind?" said Tom, obviously pleased with the way things were going.

"Okay," said Bill, "you talked me into it. I'll change my mind."

He grabbed the glass with all the oil on top.

"Hey, wait a minute," Tom protested, and there was genuine

terror in his voice. "You don't want that one. If you look clost, you can see it's loaded with oil. Here's the one you want."

But it was too late. Bill drank orange juice and salad oil. "Delicious," he grinned. "Positively delicious."

Tom looked with distaste at the glass he was holding. He managed a smile, but it was a weak one.

"Good boy, Bill," he muttered finally.

"Am I in the Club for drinking my medicine, Tom?"

"I guess so."

"For a thousand years and four days?"

Tom nodded glumly.

"Are you going to drink yours now, Tom?"

He nodded again.

"And are you going to drink a glass with Lillian, Fred, Dan, Jack, Bob and Jane, like you promised?"

Tom looked around him. The girls were biting their lips to keep from laughing. Frank had buried his head in his pillow.

"Drink it," said Bill.

"It's delicious," said Ernestine. "Ast Anne."

If looks could have killed, the Princess's body would have been in an advanced stage of rigor mortis.

"Ast Ernestine," said Martha.

"Ast Martha," said Frank.

"Ast Frank," said Bill.

"I don't know why I work here," Tom shook his head dully. "Seventeen years with the family, and when I start to get a little old they try to poison me. A hundret and twenty million people in the country, and I got to be the one who works here."

"No," said Anne. "Don't drink it, Tom. It was only a joke, and not a very good one, I guess. We're sorry, Tom."

Tom stepped back with dignity, favored us with a withering glance, and drained his glass. Then he stalked out of the

room, descended to the kitchen, and returned with the bottle of castor oil and a spoon. He handed them to Ernestine, and he didn't forget to bow.

"Here, Doochess," he said. "I know who put him up to it. I seen that guilty look. I ain't deef, you know. I ain't blind. Now you get the rest of them to take their medicine, like the doctor said."

He left the room again, only this time he backed out, bowing, curtsying, and grasping his forelock.

Ernestine tried to hand the bottle to Anne, but Anne wouldn't take it.

"It's your responsibility," Ernestine said. "You're the oldest."

"Tom's right," Anne replied. "I seen that guilty look too, Doochess, so it's up to you. I delegate the responsibility."

COMPLETELY DEAD

MARTHA was red haired, freckled, and oblivious to the fact that within the last year she had grown tall, slender, and curvey—very curvey. The realization was to come in time—about the time that the freckles, with considerable prompting from Martha, started to disappear.

But for the moment she preferred blue serge bloomers to skirts, middie blouses to sweaters, and bicycles to rumble seats.

Martha was casual, easy going, steady, and a favorite with everybody. Efficiency came to her naturally, partly because of her temperament, partly because she was at the age when the mere mention of work had a depressing effect. If possible, work was to be avoided altogether. If not, it was to be disposed of as rapidly as possible, and with a minimum of fatigue. Hence, efficiency.

She had just finished her sophomore year in high school, during which she had broken Anne's and Ernestine's previous records by carrying home her own books less than a dozen times. She accepted her male carriers matter-of-factly, without attributing their attention to anything going on under her very nose. Our house was almost two miles from Montclair High School, and Anne and Ernestine used to say that Martha selected her gentlemen friends solely on their ability to carry heavy weights for long distances.

We recovered from chicken pox in a comparatively short time, and Martha took over the job of supervising the packing for Nantucket. She had Frank and Bill bring three trunks from the attic to the upstairs hall. We carried our clothes to her, and she made sure we had everything we needed before she let us put them in the trunks. Martha herself was established in a comfortable chair, and didn't have to move.

To simplify the matter of logistics, Martha had drawn up a number of check-off lists, from which she seemed to derive more than her share of satisfaction. Martha usually was on the receiving end of orders from Anne and Ernestine, and it was a special pleasure for her to have an opportunity to boss them now.

"Name!" she began by asking Anne, when Anne appeared in the hall with a pile of her own clothes. "Speak out loudly so I can hear you."

"My cow," Anne replied. "It's all right to be efficient, but don't carry it too far."

"Do you," said Martha, offering to hand her the check-off lists, "want to supervise the packing?"

Anne admitted she didn't.

"Then be good enough, please, just to answer a few simple questions. Name!"

"Paavo Nurmi, the Flying Finn," Anne told her. "Age, eighteen. Hobbies, taking orders and impudence from a mere slip of a girl."

"Speak out loudly so I can hear you," Martha said, thumbing

through her papers and coming up with Anne's check-off sheet.

"Oh, what's the use," Anne snorted. And then, shouting, answered: "Anne."

"Good," Martha beamed. "Dresses?"

"Six."

Martha made a note of it. "Bathing suit?"

"Sure does, Mr. Bones. Suits just fine."

"Speak out loudly so I can hear you."

"One," Anne hollered. "You're so efficient, I'll bet you're rocking with the grain of the wood."

After running through the complete list, all the way from hairpins to shoe trees, Martha directed Anne where to stow her clothes. Then the rest of us, by ages, stepped up, gave our names, and went through the same routine.

Each older child, besides being responsible for himself, was responsible for a younger child. Anne was responsible for Jane, Ernestine for Jack, Martha for Bob, and Frank for Dan. This applied not only to packing clothes, but any family project or emergency. In the event of fire, or when crossing a street, or when it came to writing up the daily jobs on the process charts, the older ones were supposed to help their particular charges. Bill, Lillian, and Fred were in the intermediate group —old enough to look out for themselves, but not old enough to help anyone else.

Once the clothes were packed, together with sheets, blankets, tools, dolls, games, scrapbooks, crystal detectors and headphones, stamp collections, free samples and other articles that couldn't possibly be left behind, we devoted our attention to Departure Day.

Martha, meanwhile, had taken over the budget. Martha was not ungenerous with her own money, although it didn't exactly flow through her fingers. But when it came to handling

Mother's money, her fingers had to be pried apart and twisted. It was a waste of time to tell Martha that you can't take it with you. She had long since made up her mind that, if that were the case, no sensible person would even dream of going.

She drew up requisition slips that we had to fill out in triplicate to buy anything for the house or to get our weekly allowances. We agreed with Bill that it seemed a lot of trouble to go to for fifteen cents a week.

To get to Nantucket, we planned to take a Lackawanna train from Montclair to Hoboken, a ferry from Hoboken to New York, a night boat from New York to New Bedford, Massachusetts, and the Nantucket boat from New Bedford to our destination. We knew that the transferring, with all our suitcases and the younger children, was going to be a job. But the trip on the night boat was cheaper than going to New Bedford by train.

Martha, who had been duly identified by Anne at the bank, cashed a check and went to New York to pick up the reservations. She was appalled and unnerved when the man at the ticket office on the dock told her the total cost.

"There must be some mistake," she told him. "It's Nantucket we're going to, not Paris, France. Would you mind adding it up again?"

The man added again, and then Martha checked him—twice. When she finally became convinced that there was no mistake, she decided to turn back two of the five staterooms Mother had reserved, and to exchange two of the full-fare tickets for half fares.

When she returned from the city, Martha, bristling with indignation, told Ernestine and Anne about the prices. She also explained about turning in the staterooms and exchanging the tickets.

"So I saved better than twenty dollars," she concluded. "There'll have to be four of us in each of two staterooms, and three in the other."

"Good night," said Anne, "even three persons in one of those staterooms is a slum. But I guess we'll manage somehow."

"Of course we will," Martha agreed. "And think of saving . . ."

"Wait a minute," Anne interrupted. "You've forgotten all about Tom. Where's he going to sleep?"

"And if you try to tell us he can sleep in one of our staterooms," Ernestine put in, "all I can say is that's carrying economy a little too far."

"It certainly is," Anne agreed. "The very idea!"

"I'll scrub floors," Ernestine announced dramatically. "I'll clean out the rest rooms in the Hudson Tubes. But I will not . . ."

"Neither will I," said Anne.

"I didn't forget about him," Martha insisted. "And for cat's sake put down those scrub brushes and get up off your hands and knees."

"Where's he going to sleep then?" Anne asked.

"Well," said Martha, "he was complaining just the other day about how he never slept a wink on the way to Nantucket. So if he doesn't sleep anyway, what's the use of throwing away perfectly good money?"

"You can't do that to him," Anne protested. "You go right back to New York and get another stateroom."

"It's all right," Martha insisted. "I already told him about it."

"Poor Tom," Anne sympathized. "What did he say?"

"Oh, you know Tom. He grumbled about a hundred and

twenty million people in the country, and about how Lincoln freed all the slaves but one. But he didn't really object."

"Poor Tom!" Anne repeated. "My cow."

"I don't know why he puts up with us," Ernestine agreed.

"Look," said Martha, fishing angrily in her pocket for the checkbook. "Do either of you want to take over the budget? I ask you, do you?"

"I guess it wasn't such a bad idea after all," Anne hastily assured her.

"And you did," Ernestine pointed out, "save more than twenty dollars of Mother's money."

"Perfectly good money," amended Martha, who obviously considered all currency of the realm to be eminently satisfactory. "And I wouldn't have done it if he hadn't said he didn't sleep."

"It's all right, I guess," said Anne, "but how about those two half fares?"

"What about them?" Martha demanded belligerently, fishing for the checkbook again.

"Put that thing away," Anne told her. "I'm in charge here, and I'm not going to have checkbooks, check-off sheets, manifests, or bills of lading waved in my face every time I open my mouth."

"Frank might possibly be able to get away with a half-fare ticket, but not you," Ernestine said.

"I'd like to know why not," Martha replied indignantly. "I'm a little tall, I admit. But I certainly can bend my knees when I go up the gangplank."

"It's not just your being tall," Ernestine said significantly.

"Well, what is it then?"

"For goodness' sake," said Anne, looking. "Just look at yourself."

Completely Dead

Martha glanced down and shrugged. "Oh, that," she said. "My gosh, nobody pays any attention to things like that."

Our train for Hoboken left in the early afternoon. We didn't want to have to pay for more than one taxicab, so five of the older children, with Ernestine in charge, walked from the house to the station. Anne and Tom, with the five youngest children and all of our suitcases, waited at the house for a taxi.

The suitcases were lined up on the front steps, and Anne had the five children washed and ready, when the cab finally appeared.

It wasn't until the suitcases were stowed away and the children packed into the taxi that Anne discovered Tom was missing. She called him, but he didn't answer. She unlocked the front door and searched the house. In the kitchen she found Tom's cap, a cage with our two canaries, and an empty cardboard box with holes punched in the top. But no Tom.

The cab driver kept blowing his horn, and Anne went out front to pacify him. The children were jumping and crawling around the car, and Bob was sitting in the driver's lap.

"If you're the ringmaster," the driver told Anne, reaching into the back seat and rescuing his hat from Jack, "you'd better get this show on the road. I've got other stops to make this afternoon, you know."

"I'm doing the best I can," Anne said. "We'll be ready in a minute. I think our cook is looking for his cat."

"How about Mr. Chairman?" Fred asked.

Anne snapped her fingers. "I knew I forgot something. Where is he?"

Mr. Chairman was our dog, a sort of collie. He was there, barking at the cab and growling at the driver.

[37]

"Get a leash on him," Anne told Fred. "Don't let him get away."

Tom came running down Eagle Rock Way.

"Fourteen," he panted, "ain't nowhere to be found."

"We'll have to leave her," Anne said. "We're late for the train right now. Get into the cab, quick."

"Leave Fourteen?" Tom asked incredulously. "Are you crazy?"

"Please. We simply must catch the train."

"What do you think I am," Tom snapped. "I ain't going to leave that cat. If she don't go, I don't go."

"We've got Mr. Chairman," Anne begged. "And you've got the canaries."

"But I ain't got Fourteen."

"Damn it," Anne shouted. "I've planned this trip for better than two weeks. I planned it right down to the last bath and shined shoe. A plague of chicken pox didn't delay it and no cat is going to ruin it. Now get into that cab."

Tom never had heard Anne swear before, and he was impressed.

"I ain't even got my cap," he said. "Nor the birds, neither."

"Go get them," Anne told him, "and be damned quick about it."

"You heard what the lady said," the driver put in. "I got other stops to make."

Tom went, mumbling but hurrying. "I wisht your father could hear you talk like that. He'd learn you. He'd learn you good, you bold thing you."

Tom was still mumbling when he returned in a joggling half run, with his cap and the cage, and got into the cab. "He'd learn you, all right. Swearing like a cab driver in front of all them children. You ain't too big to spank, neither."

Anne locked the front door and jumped into the cab.

"One cab for seven people, eight suitcases, a dog and two canaries," the driver inventoried as we started down the driveway. "You should have ordered three at least."

"We're not too crowded," Anne said as cheerfully as she could.

"Is that dog housebroken?"

"Usually," Anne lied.

"I don't think my insurance covers this."

"It probably does," she laughed weakly, "if you have an act-of-God clause."

A block from the house, we saw Fourteen. The cab stopped, Tom called, and there was a streak of orange as the cat dived into his lap and then perched on his shoulder.

"Look at that," Tom crowed, all of his complaints forgotten. "She was waiting on us. Smartest cat I ever seen, bar none."

"Are there any other passengers or livestock we are supposed to pick up?" the driver asked.

"No," Anne told him sheepishly.

"No cows, goats, or other children?"

"No."

"You sure we got them all?"

"Yes."

"And may one inquire where the destination is at?"

"Oh, excuse me," said Anne. "The Lackawanna station."

"I thought maybe it was Overbrook. You know, the Funny Farm."

"No," Anne said meekly. "The Lackawanna station. Please."

She leaned back in the seat and tried to adjust Jane a little more comfortably on her lap. She closed her eyes and thought of Mother, now safe in England. She thought of previous trips, when we had driven to New Bedford and taken the Nantucket boat from there. She thought of Dad—strong, gay, and dependable—sitting behind the wheel of our old Pierce Arrow, blowing his bulb horns and shouting "road hog" at the drivers who swerved for their lives as we went barreling by in a cloud of smoke.

From Anne's standpoint, at least, the remainder of the trip to Nantucket had only about half the earmarks of a howling success—the howling half.

The hubbub of the night-boat dock demoralized Mr. Chairman, and he yapped, howled, and had to be dragged stiff-legged along the dock and to the gangplank.

Every two or three steps, Frank would stop and bat him to try to keep him quiet, but the wallops only made Mr. Chairman yap and howl all the louder.

Tom, with Fourteen and the bird cage under one arm and a bulging wicker suitcase under the other, kept shouting threats about how he'd dose the dog good if he didn't shut up.

Each of the older children held the hand of his particular younger charge, and carried a suitcase. Martha discouraged eager porters, who came running to meet us, by telling them we were too poor to afford them.

By the time we single-filed up the gangplank, which Martha negotiated almost on her knees, the rails were lined with grinning spectators. Anne and Ernestine looked straight ahead, pretending not to notice, but the rest of us waved and grinned back.

"Carry your bags?" said a porter who was coming down the gangplank from the ship.

"No," shouted Frank, who sometimes read *College Humor,* "let them walk."

That was the sort of joke that appealed to Tom, and he

laughed deafeningly, through his nose as always. "Henc, henc, henc, henc," he cackled. "That's a hot one."

The purser was so engrossed by our entrance that he made no pretense of checking to see whether we had enough full-fare tickets. He did insist, though, that Mr. Chairman and Fourteen be checked with the freight, down in the hold. All through the night you could hear Mr. Chairman complaining about that.

We were allowed to keep the birds, and they ended up in Anne's stateroom, where she shared the lower berth with Jane, while Fred and Dan shared the upper. Anne wouldn't let either Jane or Dan drink any liquids after six o'clock, but the inevitable occurred anyway.

It wasn't until the following morning, when we had transferred at New Bedford to the Nantucket boat, that Anne discovered Morton Dykes.

Morton was an Amherst man, and a sheik whom Anne rated high on her hit caravan. He was very tall—six feet seven or eight—and thin, but quite good looking in his patent-leather hair and Oxford bags. He and Anne had had a good many dates that spring, while she was at Smith. We had often heard her talk about him, but never had seen him before.

It wasn't necessary to check animals with the freight on the Nantucket boat. Morton bumped into Anne on the upper deck, where all of us—including the birds, dog, and cat—were gathered.

Bumped is the word, because it soon became apparent that, so far as Morton was concerned, the meeting was not only unpremeditated and unrehearsed, but undesired.

"For goodness' sake," said Anne, trying to straighten out her dress, which had been rumpled beyond repair by Jane, "Look who's here. Hello, Morton."

"Hello," Morton almost whispered, edging away as if Anne had something he didn't want to catch. "Good to see you."

"Good to see you, too," said Anne enthusiastically. When Anne was enthused, her voice had all the modulation of a cheer leader's in the last minutes of the final quarter. Morton edged still further away. "I knew you and your Mother were coming to Nantucket," she added, "but I had no idea we'd be on the same boat."

"We were on the night boat with you, too," Morton reported resentfully. "We saw you come aboard."

"Oh, you did?" was all Anne could manage.

"Was that your dog that howled all night?"

"I didn't hear anything," Anne said.

Morton edged some more, and Anne finally realized that he didn't want to be mistaken for one of our group. The realization made her furious.

"Come on over," she said, "and meet everybody. Pull up a chair and make yourself at home."

"No thanks. I've got to run."

"Why don't you bring your Mother up here, and we'll all sit together?"

The suggestion caused Morton to drop all pretense of edging, and to break into an open retreat.

"See you around," he whispered over his shoulder.

"Or," Anne hollered after him, "we could all come and sit with you."

Morton disappeared down a ladder to the lower decks.

"So that's Morton Dykes," Ernestine said. "Gee, he's cute —and so tall. The least you could have done was introduce me."

"I tried," Anne told her bitterly. "You heard me try."

"The whole boat heard you," Martha said. "If you ask me, he's a beanpole and a wet smack."

"You're just judging him as a potential book carrier," Ernestine grinned. "You know those tall, thin ones get tired easily."

"He seemed to be in a hurry to get somewhere," Martha said. "Does he always edge that way, like a crab?"

"He was ashamed of us," said Anne. "Well, any feeling I may have had for him in the past is dead. Completely dead."

"Why would anyone be ashamed of us?" Bill wanted to know. "You girls are crazy. He looked to me like he had heard about our chicken pox, and he hasn't had them."

"Martha's right," Ernestine agreed. "He is a wet smack."

"Dead," Anne repeated dramatically. "Completely dead."

5

MOTHER'S BATHING SUIT

ALL of us, but especially Anne, were glad to see our cottage at Nantucket.

Dad had named the cottage The Shoe, in honor of Mother, because he said she was like the old lady who lived in one. The Shoe was flanked by two circular lighthouses, which Dad had bought years before from the government. One lighthouse had been used by Dad as a study, and the other by us as an overflow dormitory.

We wondered how Nantucket was going to be without Dad. He had left his mark on every room in The Shoe. There were the dot and dash messages he had painted on the ceilings over our beds, the summer he decided we should learn the Morse code. There were the astronomical diagrams he had painted billboard fashion on the dining-room walls, showing the size of the earth and other planets, as compared with big stars. There were photographs of nebulae and constellations that had been given Dad by Harvard University, and which he had hung only two feet from the floor, so that even the smallest children could see them.

We went from room to room, looking at everything and finding it good.

The trunks had followed us from the express office at the dock. Martha opened them in the dining room, found a comfortable chair, and started giving us instructions about unpacking them.

Everyone came and got his clothes, and put them in the bureaus. Tom fed the animals and cleaned the kitchen. Frank and Bill put up the screens. Anne and Ernestine swept away a winter's accumulation of sand.

"That's the most efficient house opening we ever had," Anne told us when we were through. "Everyone did a fine job, particularly Martha on the packing."

"Martha is Dad all over again," Ernestine agreed. "She's naturally efficient."

Martha grinned happily, pushed herself up from her chair, and started over to the trunks to get her own clothes. Someplace between the chair and the trunks, a terrible realization struck her. She knew the trunks would be empty, and they were. She knew, too, there wasn't any use asking if anyone had picked up her clothes by mistake.

"Don't anybody ever say I'm efficient again," she squealed.

"Of course you're efficient," said Anne. "Stop fishing for any more compliments. I just finished saying you did a fine job on the packing, and we've got everything we need."

"We haven't got my clothes or bathing suit," Martha shouted, "and we need those. I haven't got a stitch except what I've got on my back."

"Nonsense," Anne said. "They must be around someplace. Who took Martha's clothes?"

[46]

Mother's Bathing Suit

Martha shook her head, and she was near tears. "No use to look. I remember now. I didn't pack them."

"But the check-off lists?" Anne asked. "How could you forget your own clothes?"

"I don't know."

"You sure you didn't pack them?"

"The check-off lists were for everybody else," Martha said. "Since I was doing the packing, there wasn't any use to have one for me."

"Oh, Lord. That means we'll have to get you a whole new outfit."

"No we won't," Martha insisted. "The budget can't stand it. I'll go around in a barrel first."

The boys started giggling, and Anne and Ernestine couldn't help but join in. Bill sat down in the chair Martha had vacated, and made believe he was thumbing through a sheaf of papers.

"Name?" he asked Martha.

"Speak out so we can hear you," said Frank.

Martha managed a sick grin. "Mud," she said. "I admit it. Age, almost fifteen. Favorite pastime, eating crow."

Anne still wanted Martha to go down to the village and buy some clothes and a bathing suit, but Martha was determined not to waste the money.

"I just need some things to bum around in," she said. "I'm not a boy-crazy flapper, trying to impress an Amherst man. I'll find something."

Anne and Ernestine agreed they'd hand her down some clothes, and Frank said he'd hand up a sweatshirt, some jerseys, and a pair of dungarees.

"Swell," Martha said. "I don't have to worry about a bathing suit because I can wear Mother's until she gets here. And I'll write her to be sure to pick up my suit when she stops by Montclair."

"I can see you in Mother's suit," Ernestine scoffed. "Why it's practically a Gay Nineties model."

"Who cares about that?" Martha said. "All I want is something to cover me. You two make me sick."

Mother wasn't a swimmer and didn't like the water. She did occasionally wade in up to her knees, splash some water on her shoulders, duck down almost to her elbows, and then hurry home. If she met any of us en route to the beach, she'd inform us, through blue lips and chattering teeth, the surf that day seemed particularly refreshing. The waves on the bathing beach never got more than a foot high during a full gale, but even in a flat calm it was surf to Mother.

Mother's suit left nothing exposed. Even Dad, who insisted that the girls wear black, old-fashioned models, had to admit that Mother carried modesty a little to the extreme, and that she seemed to put on more than she took off when she prepared to go in the water.

Her suit had numerous appurtenances, including a sash and a bandanna. But its two principal components were a black undergarment, that started with a hug-me-tight neck and ended several inches below the knees, and a huge, long, black, billowing outergarment, that Dad said might be useful to Barnum and Bailey if it were dyed khaki. The outergarment had long sleeves and hung down to Mother's ankles, which themselves were encased in black cotton stockings and high bathing shoes.

"Mother's suit is out of the question," Anne told Martha. "You'd look completely ridiculous in it."

"If it's good enough for Mother," said Martha, "it's good

enough for me. You ought to be ashamed of yourself, talking about her clothes like that."

"It's not her clothes that are ridiculous," Anne said. "A few years ago, everybody wore suits like that, and a good many people Mother's age still do. But it would look ridiculous on you."

"It's not much more ridiculous than the suits Dad made us wear," Martha protested. "We have to wear a black thing underneath, and sort of dresses, too."

"I know it," Anne admitted. "But at least ours end at the knees and have short sleeves."

It had taken Anne years to get Dad to allow her and the other girls to bob their hair and wear short skirts, silk stockings, and teddies. Dad hadn't approved of the style trends that had set in since the war. He said they were purely temporary, that girls eventually would come to their senses, and the fact that everyone else dressed that way made no difference. He had refused to yield any more than the sleeves and a couple of inches around the hems of the girls' swimming outfits. It was a sore point with the two oldest girls.

Martha kept insisting to Anne that she would look all right in Mother's suit, and Anne finally gave in.

"All right," Anne said. "If you don't care how you look, I suppose I don't. And since none of us should go out with boys until Mother gets here, I guess you can't do Ernestine and me any permanent damage."

Frank, Bill, and the younger children already had on their suits, and the two boys took the younger ones down to the beach, which was only a couple of hundred yards from the cottage. Martha said she'd slip on Mother's suit and join them. Anne and Ernestine had to finish sorting sheets and blankets, and told Martha they'd be down in about half an hour.

It was late afternoon when the two oldest girls finally reached the beach. Both of them were tired from the journey to Nantucket and the housework. They sighed with relief as they sank down in the warm sand, where all of us but Martha were sitting. Martha was the best swimmer and diver in the family, and could stay in the water for hours without getting cold.

"This is the life," said Anne stretching herself contentedly. "This is what I've been dreaming of ever since the chicken pox. I think everything is going to be much simpler from now on."

"Will you take me out over my head?" Jack asked her. "Frank took us in but he won't take us over our heads."

"In a little while," Anne agreed sleepily. "I just want to get a little of what sun's still left." She lay down flat on her back. "Will someone make that dog stop shaking sand all over me?"

Frank leaned over and whacked Mr. Chairman, but it didn't do any good.

"Nobody ever takes me out over my head," Jack complained.

"Where's Martha?" Ernestine asked. "Out at the raft?"

Frank nodded.

"How does she look in Mother's suit?"

"Man, she looks grand," Frank said enthusiastically. "You ought to see her."

"I'll bet," Ernestine smiled. "Miss Atlantic City of 1890."

"She's out there," said Frank, "with that tall, skinny man we saw on the boat."

Anne sat up suddenly, now wide awake.

"Morton Dykes?" she said. "You mean he's seen Martha in that outfit. My cow! What will he think of us now?"

"What do you care?" Ernestine grinned. "Your feeling for him is dead, remember?"

"Completely dead," Bill echoed.

Mother's Bathing Suit

"He doesn't seem to mind the way her suit looks," Frank said. "Every time she dives, he helps her back on the raft. You'd think she was crippled or something."

Anne shaded her eyes and looked out toward the float. It was easy to pick out Morton, because he stood almost a foot taller than anyone else. But at first she couldn't spot Martha.

"I don't see anyone in Mother's suit," she said. "It ought to be conspicuous enough."

Then a trim, curvey, black-clad figure hit the springboard and went into a beautiful jackknife that was unmistakably Martha's. A red head emerged from the water and a hand waved casually to the tall boy on the raft, who waved back vigorously. There was a wake of spray as Martha Australian-crawled back to the beach.

"Where did she get *that* suit?" yelled Ernestine, who had seen the dive too. "What would Dad say?"

"What will Mother say?" Anne asked.

Martha blew water out of her nose, tossed the hair out of her eyes, and started up the beach to join us. Frank and Bill, clicking their tongues as loudly as if they were a couple of Decency Leaguers who had stumbled into a nudist camp, ran to her with towels. They made a great pretense of turning their heads away, and of hiding their eyes with their hands.

The beach wasn't very crowded at that time of day, but those who were there were sitting up and watching.

"You boys stop that," Anne stage-whispered. "I'm ashamed of you!"

"Here, Martha, quick," Frank said, pretending not to hear. "Drape these towels around you. If you hurry, the beach police-man may not even notice."

"Besides," said Bill, "we don't want you to catch pneumonia."

"Would you two," Martha inquired good naturedly, pushing them and the towels aside, "like a good punch in the nose?"

She sank down nonchalantly in the sand between Anne and Ernestine, and attempted to even old scores with Mr. Chairman by shaking her wet hair at him. "Boy," she said, "the water's really the cats."

She didn't seem to notice Anne's and Ernestine's frigid stares.

"Saw a friend of yours out there," she told Anne. "What a wet smack. You ought to see him in a bathing suit. More of a beanpole than ever."

Martha was wearing what appeared to be a tight-fitting black union suit. If you looked at it closely, you could tell it was the under part of Mother's suit, with the legs and sleeves rolled up as far as they would roll. It wasn't any more extreme than bathing suits other girls were wearing, but Anne and Ernestine were shocked almost beyond words.

"Go back," Anne finally whispered to her, "and get the outer half of it. The idea!"

"And," said Ernestine, "roll down those legs."

Jack still wanted Anne to take him out over his head, but she didn't hear him.

"I blush for you," Anne told Martha. "What will Mother say?"

"What have I done now?" Martha asked. "What's this all about?"

"You know perfectly well," said Anne, "so don't try to act so innocent."

"If you mean that sheik of yours, you don't have to worry. He's a wet smack who always wants to help you up on the raft. I'm wise to him."

"Let's leave Morton out of the conversation," said Anne.

Mother's Bathing Suit

"I never saw anybody so jealous," Martha complained. "Why I wouldn't touch your ten-foot beanpole with a pole."

"He's not my ten-foot beanpole," said Anne. "And I'm not talking about him. I'm talking about that bathing suit."

"You said it was all right to wear it."

"I said it was all right to wear all of it. Not just the under half."

"You didn't think I was going to wear the outer part too, did you?"

"Of course we did," Ernestine said. "You know perfectly well we did."

"So that's what you meant when you said I'd look ridiculous." Martha started to laugh. "I can see myself in that black tent, can't you? I don't wonder you thought everyone would stare at me. Why I couldn't swim a stroke in that sea anchor—you should have known that."

"Martha," said Ernestine. "Listen, Martha. It's not decent. You shouldn't walk out of your boudoir in that thing. Here, take this towel, dear."

"We could bury her with sand until everyone goes home," Fred suggested hopefully.

"It shows every curve," Anne said. "It leaves nothing to the imagination."

"I'm getting tired of being bossed," Martha hollered. "Always thinking about how you look, and never thinking about how you swim. Besides, there's nothing to imagine."

Anne was patient. "You know Dad's rules for girls in this family. Modesty, Martha. Modesty."

"But nobody wears two-piece suits any more. You think you're flappers, but you don't realize that times have changed. I've got a right to live my own life."

"You know the rules as well as we do," Anne continued.

[53]

"Two-piece bathing suits. Skirts at least to the knees, black stockings, and a minimum of skin showing. What would Mother say?"

"I'll bet," said Martha, "she'd say times have changed and that I could wear the same kind of suit other girls are wearing. And I'll bet, when she said it, you two would race each other downtown to get one-piece suits."

"That shows," Anne announced, "how well you know Mother."

"Yes, sir," Martha nodded, obviously deriving a good bit of satisfaction from the mental picture, "when she said it, it would be 'on your mark, get set, go.' "

"But she wouldn't say it," Anne insisted. "She'd die if she saw you like that."

"All right," Martha surrendered. "You're the boss, and I've got to do what you say. I'll wear the rest of it. But I'm going to take a hem of at least a foot in the bottom. And I positively draw the line at black stockings this summer."

Martha got up and, disdaining the offer of towels, headed back toward the cottage. There was no doubt that Mother's suit never looked better.

"I think," Ernestine told Anne, "that we could all do without black stockings. No one else wears them."

Anne nodded. "I was thinking the same thing. As Martha says, times do change. Even Dad probably would admit that. Probably."

"And you know she did look mighty cute in that one-piece job."

"I suppose she did," said Anne. "In a childish sort of way, of course."

"That's what I mean—in a childish sort of way. And it must be much easier to swim when you have just one piece."

Mother's Bathing Suit

"I guess it is," Anne agreed. "Lord knows I don't like the idea of two-piece suits any better than she does—if as well. But you know I can't repeal any rules behind Mother's back and— Hey, wait a minute. Who's side are you on, anyway?"

"Yours," Ernestine said, "I suppose. I wasn't going to take off the outer part of my suit, honest! Just the stockings."

Anne shaded her eyes and looked out at the float again. The tall thin figure was still there.

"Will you take me out over my head now, Anne?" Jack asked. "Nobody ever takes me out over my head."

"I guess so," said Anne, putting on her bandanna and shaking the sand from between the two layers of her outfit.

She took Jack by the hand and Ernestine took Bob. They started slowly into the water.

6

BEATING THE RAP

TOM complicated matters about a week later by being haled into police court. Without offering any excuses for Tom, it might be pointed out that he was an Irishman of strong prejudices—particularly against the British.

Tom's mood had been black for several days because a nearby family had brought an English cook to Nantucket, and she had been welcomed into his group.

From previous years, Tom knew most of the help in the houses near our cottage, and they'd meet in the afternoons on the beach. Partly because of his seniority and partly because he was always good company, Tom was one of the acknowledged leaders of the group. He was now torn between giving up the group altogether, or accepting the English woman. He was reluctant to do either.

She was immensely stout, stately, quiet, and dignified. She spoke with a decided British accent, and wore a light green, one-piece bathing suit, neither of which Tom approved.

Beating the Rap

Tom would join the group on the beach in the afternoons, but sit as far from the English woman as possible.

"This island is being ruint by too many Limeys," he'd tell his friends loudly. "We're thinking of going someplace else, after this summer."

If a good-looking young girl walked past in a one-piece suit, Tom would announce:

"Now there's the kind that ought to wear a suit like that. The big fat ones ought to cover up all they can, or else stay home altogether."

The British cook, who could take a hint, ignored him. Tom didn't want to be friends, but he hated to be ignored, and her snubs and accent had an accumulated effect of irritation.

One day Tom got up off the sand and started for the water, just as the cook, who was standing, leaned over to unlace a sneaker. Her tremendously plump rear, hugged protestingly in the nether portion of the suit, emerged like a conch from the shell of her half skirt. Tom almost butted into it.

She seemed to be having trouble with the sneaker, and Tom contemplated the vast expanse with loathing.

On impulse, he picked up a sizable piece of driftwood and walloped her as hard as he could.

The stick was wide and flat, and it met flesh with a sharp, resounding crack. The cook toppled over, ostrich fashion. Everyone—including Tom, who was as surprised as anybody— was too shocked to say a word. He stood there sheepishly, with the board dangling from his hand, and for one of the few times in his life he actually blushed. Both Frank and Bill, who were witnesses, swore to it.

Finally, Tom dropped the board and helped her up.

"I'm sorry," he told her. "Even for a Limey, there ain't no excuse for it. I seen it there, and I don't know why I done it."

The cook was expressionless, as she got slowly to her feet, brushing sand out of her mouth and hair. She looked right through Tom, as if he didn't exist.

"Ain't no excuse for it," Tom repeated. "First time I ever done anything like that. Ast any of these people."

She still didn't notice him.

"Here," said Tom, getting the stick, "I'll lean over and you hit me. Hit me as hard as you can."

He put the stick in her hand and leaned over, closing his eyes and hunching his shoulders to absorb the impact of the blow. When it didn't come, he straightened up again.

The cook might not have gone to the police if he had let the matter drop right there, gone on into the water, and left her alone. But Tom, who was not in the habit of walloping ladies, was sincerely mortified, and wanted to make sure he had apologized sufficiently.

"Ain't no excuse for it," he said. "I seen you stooping over and I seen the stick, and the first thing I knew . . ." The mental picture of the stick making contact with the quivering flesh came back to him, and he exploded.

"Henc, henc, henc," he cackled. "I'm sorry. I can't help it. Henc, henc, henc."

That carved it. Finally he got control of himself, and started to apologize again, but the cook stalked away, looking for the law.

Tom was summoned into court the next day, and Frank went along to bail him out, if necessary. The English cook was there, and so was most of Tom's group.

"I'm guilty," Tom told the judge. "I got no excuse for what I done."

"Why did you do it, then?"

"I don't know. She leaned over, and she was big and fat across there, and I almost walked into it by mistake. Then I seen a stick and henc, henc, henc."

"Go on," said the judge, who thought it was no time for levity. "And stop making that noise."

"Henc, henc, henc," said Tom.

Tom's laugh, although much too nasal to be pleasant, was infectious, and some of his friends joined in.

"Go on," the judge demanded sternly.

"Start from the beginning," Frank whispered. "You're laughing yourself right into jail."

Tom backed up and tried again, but he couldn't get past the stick.

"Does he always do that?" the judge asked Frank irritably.

"He never seems to get past the stick," Frank said.

"Henc," choked Tom. "I'm sorry your honor, but henc, henc, henc."

"Fifty dollars or fifteen days," the judge said, "suspended on condition of good behavior for a year, and that you apologize to this visitor to our shores."

"I'm sorry," Tom told the cook sincerely. "I honest didn't mean to do it, and I honest didn't mean to laugh about it."

"I wouldn't let you off so easy," the judge said, "except you've been coming to Nantucket for years and never have been in trouble before."

"I wouldn't of done it," Tom assured him again, "only she leaned over and . . ."

The judge rapped his gavel. "Get him out of here," he said to Frank, "before he gets to the part about the stick. Otherwise I might change my mind about suspending sentence."

Occasionally, even years later, after everyone in the family was in bed and all the lights were out, we'd hear Tom chuckling through his nose up in his bedroom. And we'd know that while he might be sorry, his regret was tempered with an intriguing mental image that would accompany him to the grave.

The remainder of the two weeks before Mother's arrival went comparatively smoothly. The economy budget stayed in balance. Ernestine had moderate success in improving the cooking. Martha looked swaddled, but eminently respectable, in Mother's shortened bathing suit. Tom didn't pick up any more sticks.

There is no denying, though, that tempers were wearing thin. Anne's pep talks were beginning to sound hollow, and fights were increasingly frequent. A steadying adult hand was needed, and most of us realized it.

There was one fight, in which the whole family took part, that started when Frank complained about the frequency with which Ernestine placed clam chowder on the menu.

Ernestine was especially fond of clams. Not only that, but we got the clams for nothing by digging them ourselves. Frank could either take clams or leave them alone, preferably the latter. He thought that clam chowder, four times in a single week, was too much to take, even under an austerity program. Sometime during the climax of the argument, Frank picked up his bowl of chowder and inverted it over Ernestine's head.

With clams draped over her ears, Ernestine arose silently, picked up her chowder bowl, and repeated the process on Frank. Fists started to fly in a mass battle that pitted the clam lovers against the clam endurers. Anne finally managed to restore peace, but not until all the chowder bowls had been emptied.

We didn't have a bathtub or a shower at The Shoe, since Dad thought bathing in salt water was more healthful, so we had to put on our bathing suits and go down to the beach to wash our hair.

By then, having let off steam, everyone was in a high if clammy good humor. There were considerable giggling, tripping, good-natured sand-throwing, and pinching as we ran down to the water. The neighbors, not being stone deaf, must have heard the threats of mutilation and death that had emerged a few minutes before from our cottage. In any event, they seemed astounded to see all of us unscathed, except for clams and potatoes in our hair, and apparently on the best of terms.

Anne deducted twenty cents from each of our allowances, which meant that some of the younger children didn't get any spending money for two weeks, and there wasn't any repetition.

Mother wrote daily, and her letters contained personal messages for each child. She could hardly wait to see Jack swim, and she was mighty proud he had learned. She certainly wouldn't forget Martha's bathing suit when she passed through Montclair. Ernestine shouldn't worry about missing her college boards—it might be best anyway for her to take a postgraduate year at high school and start college after that, when the family would be a little more settled.

Most important of all, the talks at London and Prague had gone well—very well, she thought. And she had plans for opening a motion-study school at our house in Montclair.

All of us would be on the steps, waiting for Mr. Conway, the mailman, in the mornings. There was a calendar, with a red circle around Mother's arrival date, hanging on the chimney in the dining room. Each morning at breakfast, Lillian, who was in charge of the calendar, marked off another day.

The morning before Mother's arrival, we washed and oiled the floors, waxed the furniture, polished brass, scrubbed windows, and trimmed the bayberry bushes in the front yard. Everybody, including Tom, pitched in, and when we were through the house was cleaner than it was in the beginning, is now, or probably ever shall be.

We went for a quick swim, more for sanitary reasons than for relaxation, and then put on our best clothes. Everybody looked fine, even Martha in her hand-me-downs.

Ernestine had bought a large roast for supper and spent a good part of the early afternoon telling Tom what she intended to do to him, and how she intended to torture his cat, if he charred a single inch of it. It was the first roast we had had since we left Montclair.

Lillian was stationed at the top of the taller lighthouse as a lookout for the Nantucket boat. As soon as the smoke was visible, she let us know, and Anne lined us up in the dining room for a final inspection.

"Everyone's alive and whole," she began, just as Tom stuck his head into the doorway to see what was going on, "and nobody's in jail." Tom's head disappeared again. "So I guess we did a pretty good job."

She cleared her throat and paced the floor in front of us.

"You all know," she said in her best oratorical style, "that I don't enjoy making speeches."

This was something we didn't know at all because there were few things Anne enjoyed more. Before she went to college, she had been a mainstay of the high school debating team, and drove her arguments home with such enthusiasm that her coach used to tell her she was supposed merely to stump her opponents, not tree them.

"Now that I am about to relinquish my authority," she continued, "I want to thank you one and all for your fine spirit of cooperation.

"I would caution you about three things," she said, holding up the three fingers of her right hand and counting them off one at a time. "Don't reveal to Mother about, one, Tom's being arrested; two, the disgraceful clam chowder episode; or, three, Martha's wearing insufficient clothing to the beach the day we arrived."

"What's she talking about, Fred?" Dan whispered loudly. "And why is she hollering and sticking out her arms like that?"

"Search me, Dan," Fred whispered back just as loudly.

"I'm talking about this," said Anne, forgetting her role as public speaker and leaning over so her face was on the level of theirs. "If you tell Mother about Tom and the fat woman, or about the clam chowder, or about the day Martha wore the under half of Mother's suit to the beach, I'll murder you."

"You mean," asked Fred, "the day she was naked except for that black underwear?"

"I like that!" Martha protested.

"That's just what I mean," Anne nodded. "Mother'd die if she heard it."

We started for the dock. Jane walked some of the way by herself, and then Anne and Ernestine carried her together, in a chair they made of their hands and wrists. We knew Mother would want to see all of us when her boat pulled in.

In a person's lifetime there may be not more than half a dozen occasions that he can look back to in the certain knowledge that right then, at that moment, there was room for nothing but happiness in his heart.

The walk to the boat that afternoon was one of those occasions.

The steamer rounded Brant Point and we could begin to distinguish the passengers.

"I think I see Mother," Lillian shouted breathlessly.

"Where?" we asked her. "Where?"

Lillian was too excited to tell us. "Mother," she screamed, and then jumped up and down so that Anne had to grab her dress to keep her away from the edge of the dock.

Then we all saw Mother. She was waving, and it looked as if perhaps she were jumping up and down a little too. She was still dressed in widow's clothes, but her coloring had come back. Perhaps it was just a trick of the wind, which was billowing her dress behind her and may have accounted for the jaunty angle of her hat, but she seemed stronger and more sure of herself than we had ever seen her before.

In a matter of minutes, the boat was tied to the dock and Mother was coming down the gangplank, struggling with two suitcases. Martha wasn't the only one thinking about saving tips.

People stood back and gave us room as we descended on her. First it was a mass greeting, and then we could tell that she was picking out each of us, and checking us off in her mind.

"It's so good to be home," she said. "I can't tell you how I felt when I saw all of you standing on the dock."

We said it was good to have her home. With the youngest ones hanging onto her skirts, and the rest of us trying to get as close as we could, we started walking down the dock.

"I believe all of you have grown," Mother told us, "and all of you look so tan and well!"

"You should have seen us with the chicken pox," Fred said. "We didn't look so well then."

"We were sick as dogs," Dan agreed. "And we took castor oil, too, Mother."

Beating the Rap

"That was fine," Mother said absently. "I knew you'd do . . ." She stopped dead. "Chicken pox?" she said. "What about chicken pox?"

"Didn't we write you about that?" Anne asked innocently.

"Mercy Maude," said Mother. "You know perfectly well you didn't. Who had it?"

"All of us," Anne grinned. "We got it the day you left." She turned to the boys. "You might at least have waited until Mother got home, to break the news."

"That wasn't one of the things you told us not to tell," Fred said defensively.

"You didn't have anything else did you?" Mother asked.

Anne shook her head.

"Anything else happen you didn't write me about?"

"That was the only important thing. Really!"

Mother reached out, over the heads of Bob and Jack, and squeezed Anne impulsively around the waist. Anne looked as if whatever she had been through in the last five weeks had been worth while.

Ernestine personally supervised the final stages of the roast beef, and it was red and tender. There were candles on the dinner table, and we used the good silver. No holly was to be had on Nantucket, at least in the summertime, but we decked the halls with boughs of bayberry.

Mother thought the roast beef was delicious and made a point of complimenting Tom on it.

"It ain't done quite as much as it ought to be," Tom told her, "but we got a lot of cooks around here spoiling the cloth."

"I'm afraid," Mother said to us after Tom had retired to the kitchen, "that we won't be able to have roast beef as often as we used to. That'll be all right, won't it?"

"We know it," Martha said. "You don't have to worry about that."

"We're used to substitutes," Frank put in.

"We'll have to rely a little more on less expensive things like —well, liver, cold cuts, fish, and clam chowder."

"I love clam chowder," said Ernestine glaring at Frank. "We'll have some of that real soon."

"She eats it until it comes out of her ears," Frank smirked complacently. Then imitating Tom, he laughed through his nose. "Henc, henc, I'm sorry for what I done, but henc, henc, henc."

"What's the matter, dear?" Mother asked. "Is something stuck in your windpipe? Hit him on the back, Bill."

"There's nothing the matter with him," said Bill, who obliged anyway, with all his might.

"It's just a noise he makes," Anne explained.

"Oh," said Mother, obviously relieved. "That's good. Only I don't believe I'd ever make a noise like that unless I had to, dear."

Anne thought we were skating too close to both the clam chowder and the Tom-and-stick episodes, and was eager to change the subject.

"I think it's time for Martha's surprise," she said. "What do you think Mother, we only spent $300 of the money you gave us."

"Why you couldn't have," Mother replied. "The tickets to Nantucket must have cost . . . and Martha wrote she had forgotten her clothes . . . and the milk bill . . . You didn't sell anything, did you dear?"

"That was my surprise, you speech-maker you," Martha protested. "You said I could tell her."

"That's what I want you to do," Anne said. "You were in charge of the budget, so you're the one to tell her."

"Yes, you tell me, dear," Mother nodded.

"We spent $296.05," said Martha, who always knew the bank balance to the last penny.

"I don't know how you did it," Mother told us, shaking her head. "Why if we can keep going at that rate, I know everything will be all right."

"And we've been eating like kings," Ernestine put in.

"I'd like you to help me run the house, just as you've been doing," Mother said. "And I'd like Martha to keep the budget —goodness knows I never could manage money that well."

"You'll have to make out a requisition form in triplicate when you want even two cents for a stamp," Anne warned.

"No she won't either," Martha said. "Mother's an exception. She'll only have to make out one form, and I'll fill out the two duplicates."

"Thank you, dear," said Mother. She sounded as if she meant it.

Mother had brought each of us a present. Not expensive presents, such as Dad used to bring when he returned from Europe, she explained. Just something to let us know she'd been thinking of us.

She brought out the presents while we were finishing our dessert. There were Czech dolls for Jane and Lillian, and Paris hats for Martha, Ernestine, and Anne. The girls' presents were a big success.

But the boys had trouble hiding their disappointment, when they unwrapped their packages and found that each contained a blue beret.

"All the men in France are wearing them," Mother said. "I thought you might like to start the style over here."

"They're just what we've always wanted," Frank said stoutly, trying to banish from his mind what might happen to him and Bill if they wore the berets to school.

"I guess," said Mother, "that I don't know as much about getting presents for boys as your father did. That's something I'm going to have to learn, isn't it?"

"Dad never brought anything better," Bill protested. "Just old stuff like knives and watches."

"You're good boys," Mother said. "I'll remember about old stuff like that if I go away again."

Martha asked if Mother had remembered to bring the bathing suit from Montclair. Mother shook her head.

"I had some business in New York, and couldn't spare the time to go to Montclair. So I picked you up a suit at Macy's instead." She handed Martha a package.

"If it comes below my knees," said Martha, fumbling with the wrappings, "can I take a hem in it?"

"Goodness, it won't come below your knees," Mother laughed. "It's a one-piece suit."

"One piece?" Anne and Ernestine shouted together.

"No girls wear those old-fashioned two-piece suits any more, do they?" Mother asked.

"We do," said Ernestine. "Remember Dad's rules."

"Modesty," Anne recited flatly. "Skirts at least to the knees. Black stockings. And a minimum of skin showing."

"Times change," Mother told them, "and your father would have changed with them. In most things, he was a good bit ahead of his time. I'll admit he usually stayed pretty far behind them when it came to how his daughters should dress."

Martha held up the suit. It was light blue, and had a low-cut neck.

"If you say, 'On your mark, get set, go' to me," Ernestine told her, "I'll scratch your eyes out."

"You'll have to beat me to them," said Anne. "Besides, my fingernails are longer."

Martha looked at the two oldest girls, and there was sympathy in her glance.

"I wonder if the budget couldn't stand new suits for Anne and Ernestine," she asked.

"Those old maids would be too modest," Frank put in.

The two girls didn't say anything, but they looked at Mother.

"I believe the budget can stand a knife for each of the boys," Mother said. "But I don't believe we need any more bathing suits."

She handed Anne and Ernestine each a package like Martha's.

7

BELLES ON THEIR TOES

WITH Mother home, the girls' self-imposed ban on dating was automatically lifted. Anne and Ernestine went back into circulation, hopefully rejoining their beach crowd of previous summers.

The competition was unusually stiff, because there were about three times as many girls as boys. Most of last summer's crop of males were now in college and had summer jobs on the mainland. It was apparent that in order to get rings on their fingers, belles would have to be on their toes.

Morton Dykes, besides being tall and good looking, had brought a Hupmobile roadster to the island and had rented a motorboat. So he had long since been admitted—in fact shanghaied—into the crowd. The group collected each morning, before going into the water, in a hollow formed by three sand dunes, near the Cliff Beach Bathhouse. Of all the sheiks encamped on those semi-secluded sands, Morton had amassed the largest and most eager harem.

But in spite of the manpower shortage, Anne at first wouldn't have anything to do with him.

Anne may not have been a raging beauty, but she was no strain at all upon the eyes, especially in her new bathing suit. Also, there is a possibility that Morton had become tired of having a half-dozen panting females hurrying to strike a match, every time he put a cigarette in his mouth. In any event, he did everything he could to get back in Anne's good graces.

"I don't see why you always give me the cold shoulder," he told Anne one morning, sitting down beside her on the sand.

"If I weren't a lady," said Anne, "I'd give you something that started from the shoulder. And the result would be even colder."

"I don't see what you're sore about."

"Look," Anne whispered. "There are at least fifteen beautiful women here who are dying for you to come and sit with them. Why don't you go make one of them supremely happy? And leave me alone."

"But I've just known them for a few weeks, and you and I are old buddies."

"My Buddy," Anne said sarcastically. "You'd better shove off, Buddy, before your mother sees you associating with the lower classes."

"You mean on the boat?" Morton asked. "Listen, I've been wanting to tell you about that."

"If you think there's anything to be ashamed of in a large family," Anne told him hotly, "you're a bigger wet smack than I think you are."

"And that," called Ernestine, who was sitting a few feet away, "would set a world's record."

"It wasn't your family," Morton insisted, dropping his voice so that only Anne could hear. "It was that loud-mouthed little fugitive from the old folks' home, with the cat on his shoulder."

"You're talking about the man I love," Anne warned, but

the shortage of boys was acute, and she seemed to be weakening. "We're all crazy about Tom, and he's nothing to be ashamed of."

"I hadn't heard about your father, and I never had met him. And I saw that man. And I thought . . . and, well, and Mother thought . . ."

"I don't believe you'd better tell me what you thought or your mother thought," Anne said. "I don't believe I'd consider it flattering, and I have a strong feeling that Tom wouldn't either."

"Let's forget it," Morton smiled. "Relax and have a smoke. And let's be friends, eh?"

He reached for a package of cigarettes, while a bevy of females, who hadn't missed a thing, clutched for their matches. Anne looked quickly around the tops of the sand dunes, to make sure none of her brothers were spying.

"Okay, Buddy," she grinned. "Light it for me, will you?"

He put two cigarettes in his mouth, chose among five blazing matches that were being poked into his face, lighted both smokes, and handed one to Anne. She took two long puffs and inhaled deeply.

"That's the first cigarette I've had since I left Northhampton," she said contentedly. "It tastes fine." She took another drag and inhaled again.

Ernestine, whose mouth had dropped open, watched admiringly and enviously as Anne puffed, expertly knocked off the ashes with her little finger, and finally flicked the butt over a dune.

"I didn't know you did that," Ernestine whispered, sidling over to Anne. "You go at it as if you've had plenty of experience."

"What are you talking about?" Anne asked innocently. "Go at what?"

"You know very well what I mean. Puffing away at that cigarette like a dope fiend. I didn't know you dissipated."

"There's lots of things you don't know about me. Besides, everybody smokes in college."

"Can I have one?"

"You're not in college."

"Can I just try one?" Ernestine whispered.

"I should say not. It's going to be bad enough when I tell Mother I smoke, without having to confess anything about ruining your morals."

"Anybody," Ern asked loudly, "got a ciggie?"

"Let her have one," said Morton, who had heard most of the whispering. "Here, Kid."

He tossed her his package, and a box of unused matches.

"I seem to have left mine at home," Ernestine said.

She took out a cigarette and tapped one end of it on the thumbnail of her left hand, as she had seen Morton do. Then she tapped the other end. She put it a third of the way into the center of her mouth and lighted it.

"Put that out," Anne said in her ear. "You're making a spectacle of yourself. You're supposed to smoke those things, not eat them."

No one except Anne was paying any attention.

Ernestine puffed, without inhaling, and took the cigarette from her mouth.

"That certainly," she said loudly, spitting out flecks of tobacco that were clinging to her lips and tongue, "soothes my jangled nerves. Nothing's worse than when you run out of ciggies."

"Ciggies," Anne whispered. "My cow!"

"What makes it do like that?" Ernestine asked her, contemplating the brownish, unraveled end that had been in her mouth. "It's all coming apart."

"You're supposed to hold it in your lips, not your tonsils," Anne said. "If you're going to smoke, at least wait until I show you how, and stop humiliating me in public."

Ernestine thought there was merit to that suggestion. She placed the moist fag between her thumb and middle finger, optimistically took sight on the top of the tallest dune, and flicked. The cigarette shredded open and landed six inches from her hand, where she buried it quickly in the sand.

Later that morning, on the way home from the beach, Anne told Ern she had started smoking about six months before, and had intended to break the news to Dad when she got home for summer vacation. After Dad died, she hadn't wanted to add to Mother's immediate worries, so she didn't say anything about it.

"Everybody smokes all the time at college," she said. "I didn't my freshman year, but it's hard to keep refusing them, like a wet blanket."

"Did you get the habit?" Ern wanted to know.

"Sometimes," Anne admitted, "I'd get rid of a pack a week."

"It gets a grip on you all right," Ernestine agreed. "I believe I've got the habit from that first one. I'm dying for another right now."

"You might have got the chewing habit, but I don't see how you could have got the smoking habit. You're not supposed to suck them, you know."

"I do now," Ernestine nodded. "Are you going to tell Mother about your smoking?"

"Our smoking, you mean," said Anne. And then imitating

[75]

Ern: " 'I seem to have left my ciggies at home.' *Please,* don't ever call them that again!"

"Well, are you going to tell her?"

"I suppose so," Anne admitted. "Eventually. I don't like to do anything behind her back."

She fished in the pocket of her beach coat, where there were a package of cigarettes Morton had given her, and a package of Lifesavers she had bought at the bathhouse.

"Meanwhile," she said, offering the Lifesavers to Ern, "we'd better have a couple of these."

At Mother's suggestion, the two oldest girls had moved their belongings out to one of the lighthouses, so they could sleep later in the mornings. Mother thought they were entitled to some quiet and privacy, after being in charge while she was in Europe.

In the lighthouse, Anne kept her promise that very night and taught Ernestine how to smoke. Ernestine was not a particularly apt pupil, but had a strong thirst for knowledge. The girls used up more than half of the package of cigarettes, before Anne deemed her sufficiently checked out to solo.

"And I want you to give me your word," Anne said, "that you won't smoke at least until you're in college."

"You mean not for a whole year?" Ernestine asked. "No, sir. I couldn't make any promise like that."

"Oh, one or two a week when you're out on a date or something, might be all right. But no more than that. And not where Martha and the boys can see you."

"One or two a week would be fine," Ernestine agreed. "Just enough to sooth the craving inside of me."

"We don't want to set a bad example. After all, look what happened when you saw me light one."

"I promise," Ernestine said solemnly.

The girls had kissed Mother goodnight before going to the lighthouse, which was within a few feet of The Shoe. Ordinarily, Mother went to bed about 9 o'clock, read sleepily for half an hour—her only free time of the day—and then fell asleep. She usually got up at 5:30 or 6 in the morning, to be with the younger children.

That night, for some reason, she had been restless. Reading hadn't made her sleepy. She was lonesome, and wanted company. All the younger children had gone to bed, but she saw from her window that a streak of light was coming from under the door of the lighthouse. Mother put on her bathrobe and slippers, and headed for the lighthouse to chat with the girls.

Mother thought that children were entitled to privacy, just as much as adults, and never went busting, or tiptoeing either, into anyone's room. So while several feet away from the lighthouse, she stopped and called softly.

"Girls. Andie, Ern. Yoohoo. It's Mother. May I come in?"

There was no immediate response from the interior, where the girls were ducking out their cigarettes, hiding the ash tray under Anne's bed, filling their mouths with Lifesavers, and waving towels to try to get some of the smoke out the window.

"It's Mother," she called again. "May I come in?"

"Come on in, Mother," Anne called heartily, going to the door. "I thought I heard someone calling before, but I wasn't sure."

Mother started up the steps and into the lighthouse, which was blue with smoke.

"I wasn't sleepy," she explained, "and I saw your light on. I thought I'd just come out for a visit, if you two aren't too tired. I really haven't had a good chance to talk with . . ."

The full impact of the smoke hit her as she entered the door, and she coughed.

[77]

"Something's on fire," she shouted. "Don't you girls smell it?"

"No it isn't," said Anne. "Something was on fire. It's out, now."

"Whew," whistled Mother, sitting down on Ernestine's cot. "It scared me half to death. What happened?"

"Well," Anne blushed, "I may as well tell you now. I've been smoking. I was going to tell you about it. I was going to tell you tomorrow—or the next day, anyway."

"Smoking," said Mother. "So that's it." She choked and coughed. "Why there's enough smoke in this room to nominate Mister Harding."

"I've been smoking too," Ernestine said miserably. "I was going to tell you, too."

"It's my fault, I guess," Anne said. "I taught her how."

It was obvious Mother didn't like it. Her first impulse may have been to weep, to protest, to implore, to scold. But she knew that what she said was going to be important in her future relationship with the girls. So she didn't weep, and she didn't say anything until she had taken time to think the matter through.

"In my day," she finally began, "nice girls didn't smoke. I know that's all changed. It's a mistake for me to look at it in terms of what was right in my day. I still don't approve, and it wouldn't be honest for me to make believe I did."

"You make me feel like a dog," said Anne, almost in tears. "If you want, I'll promise never to do it again."

"I don't approve of promises like that," Mother told her. "Most people smoke nowadays, and it's not right when parents make children promise not to do things that most people do."

"Besides, she might break the promise," Ernestine put in. "Those ciggies get a terrible hold on you, Mother."

"When did you find that out, dear?" asked Mother, with some concern.

"Today," said Ernestine.

"That's not so bad, then," Mother smiled. "Maybe you can even break the hold—for a couple of years, anyway."

"I could fight against it," Ernestine conceded.

"I've been trying to think up some good arguments against smoking," Mother said, "but when you analyze them, they don't seem too convincing."

She started to enumerate the arguments, counting them off on her fingers.

"If you smoke you'll have a bad reputation. I hate to let go of that one, but I'll have to admit it doesn't apply any more. It's a shame, too!

"It's bad for your health. That's open to debate. Not so bad as overeating, or not getting enough sleep.

"It stunts your growth. I doubt it, and anyway you're both grown.

"It's a filthy habit. It's not, really. Not half so filthy as gossiping or collecting old match boxes.

"It's expensive. There!" Mother beamed triumphantly. "There's a good argument. It *is* expensive, and can we afford it?"

"We don't buy them," Anne said. "Our dates always have them."

"There goes my last argument," Mother smiled, spreading her hands. "We'll just say that I don't like it, but that it's a prejudice. I don't believe in prejudices, so go ahead and light up, if you want to."

Anne fished the cigarettes and ashtray from under the bed, and offered one to Ernestine.

[79]

"Not right now," said Ernestine, whose throat and stomach were beginning to feel uneasy. "I believe my craving has been satisfied for this year—probably until I go to college."

Anne helped herself to one, lighted it, and blew self-conscious smoke rings at the ceiling.

"Where are your manners?" Mother asked. "Aren't you going to pass them to everybody? It looks as if it might be fun?"

"No, sir," Ernestine protested.

"Oh, no you don't," said Anne, putting the cigarette package behind her back. "I've led one member of the family astray today. I'm not going to be responsible for anyone else's downfall."

Reluctantly, Anne stubbed out her smoke.

"That's my last—if you'll excuse the word—'ciggie' until I get back to college," she declared. "The first thing you know, Jane might be smoking cigars. I believe it'd be safer to smoke in a nitroglycerine factory than around this house."

With Morton at her disposal, Anne's social life was pretty well taken care of for the remainder of the summer. She still didn't like him very well, but nothing better came along, and he did have a Hupmobile and a motorboat.

Ernestine searched diligently, but didn't find a man until a week before the summer was over. Then she kept him a dark secret.

His name was Al Lynch, and he had a summer job down at the grocery store, where Ern had met him when she did the shopping. He was big, hearty, loud-talking and collegiate —a little too collegiate. He wore a wooly crimson sweater which sported a green block "S" letter and a bejeweled fraternity pin as large as a fifty-cent piece.

All of us had seen Al, at one time or another, in the store, and he was not the sort of chap that one would easily overlook. Of all the sheiks on the island, his hair was the greasiest, his trousers' cuffs the widest, his fraternity pin the biggest, his football letter the flashiest, and his sweater the loudest.

He wasn't exactly handsome, but his features were perfect, and he was sure he had a way with women.

We knew Ernestine was dating somebody that last week, because she had deserted Anne's beach crowd and spent hours rolling up her hair after supper. But she didn't go out at night, and he never came to call. We didn't know until later that he worked nights checking stock, but had most of the mornings off.

Morton and four or five of Martha's ever-present and ever-neglected beaux were on the dock to see us off for Montclair. This time there was no funny business about half-fare tickets, with Mother in charge. Tom, Frank, and the pets had left a couple of days before, so that Tom could get the house opened.

Anne allowed Morton to peck her on the cheek, which Mother pretended not to notice. Martha shook hands with her boys, and even condescended to clap them on the back.

Then we noticed Ernestine and Al. They were holding hands, both hands, and looking into each other's eyes. The green "S" was still sewed securely to Al's crimson sweater, but the fraternity pin was gone.

Ernestine finally tore herself loose from him. Agnes Ayres, taking leave of Rudolph Valentino to return to the old lecher she was being forced to marry because of his money, never played the scene any better.

"Wow," shouted Bill. "Look at that hot dog in the sweater."

"Isn't that the boy who works at the grocery store?" Mother asked Anne. "How long has she been going with him?"

Half-way up the gangplank, Ernestine turned around, ran

to Al, and flung herself into his arms. Miss Ayres never played that scene any better, either.

Even Mother was too surprised and shocked to make believe she hadn't noticed *that*. Ernestine tore herself loose again, and raced radiantly up the gangplank.

"I don't think that sort of thing ought to be done in public, dear," Mother admonished her when she was safely aboard. Mother seldom took any of us to task before the other children, but it seemed time for an exception.

"Or in private either," Anne agreed. "The idea—a girl your age."

"I know it," Ernestine said, throwing back her head and looking at the clouds. "I didn't intend to do it. I tried not to do it. But there was something like a powerful magnet pulling me back to his heart."

"So that's what that green thing shaped like an 'S' is," Anne scoffed. "A magnet. Does it light up?"

"Jealousy," intoned Ernestine, still looking at the clouds, "ill becomes you, you unfortunate wench whose troth is all but plighted to a beanpole."

"Becomes me ill is right," said Anne. "Me becomes very ill —sick to my stomach."

Mother shooed the younger children away.

"I'm sure he's a lovely boy," she told Ernestine.

Anne hooted. "You can tell he thinks he's God's gift to women."

"You just can't bear to see your younger sister engaged before you are, can you?" Ernestine snapped, coming down from the clouds and looking Anne squarely in the eye.

"Engaged?" Mother almost shouted. "Do you mean to tell me that you and that . . . I'm sure he's a lovely boy," she repeated quickly.

Ernestine pulled back her topcoat, and there was the fraternity pin.

"I never saw such a big one," Anne admitted. "If you had another just like it, you wouldn't need to wear anything else above the waist. What's the fraternity?"

"Tau Tau Tau," Ernestine said proudly.

"Never heard of it. And what high school is the 'S' for?"

"You know perfectly well it's not for any high school," Ernestine hollered. "Make her stop, Mother."

"Sometimes I think I can't make any of you stop anything," Mother sighed.

"Excuse me," Anne said. "What institution of higher learning is the two-foot 'S' for?"

"Not that it's any of your business, but Al is twenty-one, and a junior at Sagiwan Agricultural and Technical College. I suppose you never heard of that, either?"

"Did you?" Anne asked.

"Everyone knows about Sagiwan Agricultural. Just because it's not full of snobs like Amherst and Harvard and Princeton."

"A Tau Tau Tau at Saggie Aggie," said Anne, shaking her head. "Saggie Aggie. It's got a catchy sound—sort of Indian, and sort of like a fat woman who needs a corset."

"I think," said Ernestine, bursting into tears, "that you're the most hateful person in the world. I really do."

"Gosh, can't you take a little kidding?"

"You and Martha both having the time of your lives all summer," sobbed Ernestine. "And finally . . . and finally . . ."

"I'm sorry," Anne choked, putting her arm around Ernestine's waist. "After all, as you say, that Morton isn't any rose. He's sure a beanpole, isn't he? And Al is cute, all right, I've got to admit that."

"Do you really think so?" asked Ernestine, blowing her nose.

"Gosh, yes!" Anne fibbed.

"Where does he live, dear?" Mother asked.

"In upper New York State. Why does everything have to happen to me, Mother?" she sniffed. "Just as vacation is over, it has to happen to me. Now I won't see him again until the Christmas holidays."

"Christmas holidays?" Mother asked.

"I'm going to meet him in New York," Ernestine said. "He's coming down especially."

"Maybe he could come to visit us during the holidays," Mother suggested.

"Could he?" Ern shouted ecstatically, hugging Mother. "Do you think he could?"

"I don't see why not," Mother said. "After all, if you're going to marry him, I'd like to meet him first."

"Oh, I guess we'll never get married," Ern said gaily. "Just engaged. Al says he's not the marrying kind. Al says why buy a cow, when milk's so cheap."

"Why, where does he think . . ." Anne began.

"It would be fine if he could come," Mother interrupted. "Much better than your meeting him in New York. He sounds, well, very interesting, dear."

"Gee, he sure is," Ernestine agreed. "Will you loan me your pen? I'm going to write him right now and invite him."

Ernestine went into the lounge, and Anne and Mother exchanged knowing glances.

"Do you know what I think?" Anne teased her. "I think you're a scheming woman. I can see right through you."

"I don't know what you're talking about," Mother grinned sheepishly.

8

SHOPPING TOUR

EVERY autumn Mother took the boys into New York on a shopping trip, to get them clothes for the coming year. This year, to save time she decided to get the shopping out of the way as we passed through the city, en route from Nantucket to Montclair.

The trip to New York was accomplished relatively painlessly. Anne took the girls, including a moon-eyed Ernestine, who almost had to be led by the hand, on to Montclair. Then Mother and the boys headed for a department store that was featuring a back-to-school sale.

Mother believed that self-expression was essential to a child's development, and always gave us a free hand in picking our clothes. She might advise, but she never vetoed.

Before leaving Nantucket, Ernestine, as chairman of the purchasing committee, had inventoried the condition of the boys' clothes, and had given Mother a list of requirements.

It was decided that each boy would get one new suit, and also would be handed down a suit from the brother immediately above him in the age scale. Frank, being the oldest and not in line for a hand-down, would get two new suits. New shirts, ties, socks, underwear and shoes—which seldom lasted long enough to be handed down—also were needed by all the boys.

Frank was in Montclair with Tom, so he wasn't included on the shopping trip. Mother thought that, being thirteen, he was old enough to get his own clothes, anyway.

In the subway on the way uptown from Barclay Street, the boys agreed that any suit bought would have to please not only its immediate possessor, but the next youngest brother who would be its ultimate owner.

It was still early when they arrived at the store, and the boys' department was nearly deserted. A middle-aged salesman, pleased at the prospect of starting the day with such a large group of potential customers, hurried up to Mother. He was precise, plump, and wore a hearing aid, which fitted over his head earphones-fashion.

"Hello there, fellows," he said heartily, in a tone designed to show that he was nothing but a great big boy himself. "Well, school's about to start, eh? I know you're all looking forward to it." He laughed and rumpled Bob's head, and Bob hid behind Mother.

"What will it be this morning?" the salesman asked Mother hopefully, "suits for all the boys?"

"Yes, please," said Mother, while the salesman, obviously figuring that this was his lucky day, beamed happily.

Mother reached into her brief-case-sized pocketbook, pulled out two blueprints, the first draft of a speech she was writing, a copy of the magazine *Iron Age,* a shawl she was crocheting for her mother, some socks she had darned on the boat, and finally her black note book. There is never anything very efficient about Mother's pocketbook.

Shopping Tour

"Let's see," she said, reading from Ernestine's list, "five suits, fifteen neckties, twenty suits of underwear, twenty-five pairs of socks, twenty shirts, and five pairs of shoes."

"Yes, Madam," smiled the salesman. It was a big, sincere smile, which was fortunate, because it was his last until the boys departed, and possibly his last for a matter of weeks.

"Do they let him play that radio when he's supposed to be working?" Dan asked Mother.

"That's not a radio, dear," said Mother, who was embarrassed but believed in answering all questions from the floor. "It's a hearing aid. So of course, it's not polite to talk about it."

"Oh, I'm sorry," said Dan, and then whispering, "What's a hearing aid?"

"He's a little deaf, dear," Mother whispered back. "So don't say anything more about it."

"What did she say?" Fred and Jack whispered to Dan.

"Deaf as a doornail," Dan whispered back. "Don't make him feel bad about it."

"If you fellows will step this way," said the salesman, "I think we can find something."

"We don't want to pay more than $17.50 for the suits," said Bill, who had been coached by the girls. "And we want them with two pairs of knickers."

Fred nudged Bill and whispered: "Deaf."

"We don't want to pay more than $17.50 for the suits," Bill shouted, as loud as he could.

"I know you don't, Sonny," the salesman said patiently. "I heard you. You don't really have to shout."

"I'm sorry," said Bill, glaring at Fred.

"Look, fellows," the man said. "It's all right about the hearing aid. Lots of boys ask about it. I'm going to show you how it works."

[87]

He explained that he kept dry cell batteries in his hip pocket, and showed the boys the volume-control rheostat in the side pocket of his coat.

"Now let's get down to business, fellows," he said, swinging out a rack of clothes. He turned to Mother. "We have a special sale on this group, Madam."

"How much?" said Bill.

"These have been marked down from $30," the salesman continued, ignoring Bill, "and they're a real buy, Madam."

"How much?" said Bill.

"They're $19.50," he admitted, glaring.

"I'm afraid that's too much, sir," Bill said. "We want something cheaper."

"I don't know, dear," Mother put in. "We might look at them, and see whether you like them."

"We don't like them," Bill shook his head. "Ernestine might not object too much, but Martha would holler. She made us promise."

"I guess you're right," Mother agreed.

"Ernestine?" asked the salesman. "Martha?"

"Ern's chairman of the purchasing committee, and Mart's in charge of the budget," Bill told him.

"I see," said the salesman, who obviously didn't, but thought it best not to pursue the subject any further.

He pulled out another rack. "These are $17," he said. "Marked down from $25. What colors did you have in mind, Madam?"

"I think we'll just let the boys pick them out," Mother smiled. "If you don't mind, would you be good enough to start with Bill—he's the biggest one; the blond."

"What color did you have in mind, young man?"

"I don't think the color will matter," Bill said.

"What kind of cloth, then?"

Shopping Tour

"I don't care about that, either. I want the kind that has buckles on the bottom of the knickers that will keep your stockings up."

The salesman looked in mute appeal at Mother, who had found a chair and was working on her crocheting.

"That seems sensible, dear," she said without looking up. "The legs of your last pair wouldn't stay up at all, would they?"

"The points on the buckle bent out of shape the first week," Bill complained. "Worst suit I ever had."

Bill went through the rack, tried on three or four suits that didn't pass the buckle test, and at last found a gray, belted model that seemed just right.

"I like this one," he said, turning around so Mother could see whether it fit.

"It fits him almost exactly," said the salesman, who was beginning to perspire a little from taking down suits and hanging them up.

Mother felt the material. "I think it's fine, dear. It should wear well, and it seems well made. It's mighty handsome, too."

The salesman was obviously relieved.

"Shall I have it wrapped?" he asked.

"Not just yet," Bill told him. "Is it all right with you, Fred?"

Fred came over, looked at it, felt it, and studied the buckles.

"Okay with me," Fred agreed.

"Does everybody have to approve it?" asked the salesman, who was becoming a little bewildered. "Are we going to have to have a vote on each suit?" he appealed to Mother.

"Oh, no," Mother assured him.

"Just this little fellow here?" the salesman asked, pointing to Fred. "Is he the one who has to approve them all?"

"Not exactly," Mother said. "It's just that the boys agreed

Fred would have to approve Bill's suit, Dan would have to approve Fred's, Jack would . . ."

"Yeeees," the clerk interrupted, looking around him furtively. "Of course. I see."

By the time the suits had been selected, the boys' department was beginning to take on the appearance of a firehouse dormitory. Coats, pants, and vests, many of them in positions just as the boys had wriggled out of them, were on chairs, tables, hooks, and the floor. The clothes racks were as culled and gaping as a turkey roost on Thanksgiving Day.

The clerk, now perspiring freely, led the boys to the underwear counter, where Mother found another chair.

"We can pay a dollar a pair," Bill told him.

"What color?" asked the salesman, who knew better now than to haggle over the price.

"You don't have to worry about that," Bill said. "The only thing we don't want is what Tom calls Indian drawers."

"Don't be Eskimo," Mother warned. "Eskimo" was Mother's word for anything that was deemed evil minded. She seldom seemed to miss a reference.

"The kind that creeps up on you," the salesman nodded morosely. "I'm dying laughing." He pulled out some boxes. "Let's see, now. Less than a dollar, any color, no Indian drawers. This has been, if I may say so, a unique experience."

"If there's anything I hate it's drawers like that, don't you, Mother?" Dan asked. "You can hardly sit still in them."

"I think," smiled Mother, burying her head in her crocheting, "you'd better pay attention to what the gentleman's showing you."

The underwear finally selected was on special sale, and was produced for inspection only after all other brands had been rejected as having Indian characteristics.

"These are just what we want," Bill said, when the specially priced goods were brought out from under a counter. "We'll take twenty pairs of them, please. Mother has the sizes."

"Only three to a customer," the salesman shook his head. "We lose money on every one of these we sell at that price."

"We certainly don't want to hurt your business," Bill agreed. "Since there are only six of us, I guess all we can take is eighteen pairs then."

The clerk, now beginning to walk as if in a trance, got the sizes from Mother and added the underwear to the growing pile of merchandise.

"To save time," he said, as we arrived at the shoe counter, "and to save me the trouble of showing you every shoe in the store, suppose you explain to me in detail, beforehand, just what it is you want in a shoe."

"The first one who says a foot," Bill warned the other boys, "is going to get in trouble with me. I think we're taking up too much of this man's time."

"I don't suppose," the salesman ignored him, "that what you'd want is what everybody else gets for their boys—a high black shoe that wears well."

"Yes," Bill nodded, "I think that's just what we do want."

"I thought maybe you didn't care about the color or whether it was high or low, just so long as the eyelets didn't rust, and the laces were genuine Western cowhide."

"Do you have any with laces like that?" Fred asked eagerly.

"No," the clerk yelled, "we don't. And I don't know whether our eyelets rust or not."

Fred was subdued. "Funny store," he whispered. "They try to sell you things they haven't got."

There was a good deal of bickering, but the boys finally decided on the shoes, shirts, ties and socks.

Shopping Tour

"I guess it's been trying for you," Mother told the salesman sincerely as she paid the bill. "But I think that buying is an important part of every child's education, don't you?"

"What's that?" he said, fumbling in his side pocket for the hearing aid switch. "I had it turned off. I can hear you now. I couldn't stand to listen any more."

"You mean," Mother asked, and the boys thought there was a trace of envy in her voice, "that all you have to do is turn a switch, and you can't hear anything at all?"

He nodded.

"It's wonderful what science can do," Mother said. There was no doubt about it. It *was* envy.

MOTHER'S SCHOOL

EIGHT of us, Ernestine down through Jack, went back to school in Montclair. Anne rode a day coach to Ann Arbor and enrolled as a junior at the University of Michigan. She joined a sorority within a few weeks and was taken into Phi Beta Kappa that spring.

Mother, besides supervising everything at home, got down to the job of trying to support the family.

The financial outlook became, if anything, even worse than Mother had expected. The big firms declined to renew their motion study contracts. Various reasons were offered. They boiled down to the belief that, while Mother might know the theory of motion study, no woman could handle the technical details of the job or command the respect and cooperation of shop foremen and workers.

The Motion Study Course, which Mother had planned while in Europe, seemed the only remaining chance. Even if industries thought she wasn't able to put time-saving theories into practice in their plants, perhaps they'd send their own engineers or other personnel to her to learn the theories, and then apply them themselves.

She mailed prospectuses to a dozen former clients and other firms that had shown an interest in motion study in the past. The course was to be held at our home in Montclair, where Dad and Mother had their offices and laboratory.

The tuition was stiff. Mother figured that if less than six firms sent representatives, she'd have to call off the whole idea. That meant we'd move to California, or accept some of the kind offers of family friends.

If there were as many as six, there still would be a chance that the family could stay together. If there were more than six, the family could stay together and there would be enough money for Ernestine to start college in the fall.

Mother wouldn't be budged on that business of sending all of us to college. When anyone tried to tell her it wasn't feasible, she jutted out her chin.

Some parents find the task of getting even one child ready for school in the morning to be an exhausting one. Mother got eight ready, saw that the beds were made and the house cleaned, supervised Ernestine's menus and Martha's budget program, kept an eye on Bob and Jane, mended and sewed on buttons, wrote Anne every day, and still found time to read aloud to us at night, to help us with our homework, and to go with us to Sunday school.

And she worked ten hours every day in the office and laboratory.

At night Mother was slow and fumbling, and there were circles under her eyes. But in the mornings her weariness was gone, and she was at her best.

Between six and seven o'clock in the mornings, she'd help the younger children make their beds and straighten up their

rooms, while listening to poems, spelling words, or multiplica-
tion tables they had been assigned to memorize for school.

At seven she waked the older ones, and then helped them
with their beds and assignments. We left for school a few
minutes after eight, and then Mother turned Bob and Jane
over to Tom, and went into her office. The stenographic staff,
which had been reduced to one, arrived at nine, and Mother
wanted to be sure Miss Butler had enough to keep her busy.

Once an hour, Mother would come out to check on Bob and
Jane. Ernestine and Martha, both of whom had been taught
to type by Dad, took turns coming home directly from school
in the afternoons and helping out in the office.

Sometimes, in spite of rules about interrupting Mother, there
were more children in the office than out of it. Miss Butler used
to say that she should have studied at a nursery school, instead
of at a business college.

None of us was supposed to enter the office without knocking, and only then when the business was urgent. We knocked,
all right, but our ideas of urgent business sometimes conflicted
with Mother's.

"Do you think," Lillian would ask, after beating a loud tattoo
on the door, "that I should wear the pink or the yellow dress
to Boodle's birthday party?"

The worst of it was that such a question would capture
Mother's interest, and she'd forget all about what she was doing.

"The yellow one is my favorite," Mother would say. "I think
those pleats on the side are precious, don't you?"

"Do you think it's long enough?"

"It is getting a little short," Mother would agree. "I'll let
the hem down after supper. How old is Boodle, anyway? It
seems to me she had a birthday . . ."

Suddenly it would dawn on her that she was being inter-

rupted. "We'll talk about it at supper, dear," she'd say firmly.
"I know it's important, and I won't forget it. But I'm very busy
right now."

She'd make a note on her desk pad about Lillian's dress, and
she wouldn't forget it.

Finally Mother devised an interruptions chart, which she
hung on the wall behind her office desk. When one of us came
into the office with a problem that wasn't vital, she'd tell the
offender:

"I wonder if you'd mind making a check by your name on
the interruptions chart? I'm trying to keep track of them, so
we can see if we can cut them down."

The interrupter would shamefacedly make his mark, while
Miss Butler grinned into her typewriter.

"Thank you, dear," Mother would say, without a trace of a
smile. "How many is that for you so far this week?"

"Eight."

"Goodness, that's nothing like Tom's. He's up to thirty
already."

Tom thought the interruptions chart was a fine idea, and
that it was a shame the way we bothered Mother when she was
trying to work.

"Keep out of that office," he'd bellow to any of us he saw approaching the door. "Ain't you got no consideration for your
poor mother? If there's anything you want to know, come
here and ast me, and I'll tell you."

"All I want to know," Ernestine said dreamily, on one such
occasion, waving a letter that had arrived from upper New
York State, "is what you'd do if the best-looking man in the
world were madly in love with you."

Tom thought that over. "I believe," he answered coyly, "that
the first thing I'd do is ast him for his frat pin. And if you're

looking for yours, you'll find it on the shelf down in the laundry."

"What's it doing down there?" Ern asked anxiously.

"It come down on your pajammers. If I hadn't of seen it, it would of ruint my wringer."

Tom considered his own appearances in the office much too vital to be classified as interruptions.

"Would you step out in the kitchen a minute, Mrs. Gilbreth?" he'd ask, sticking his head through the office door. "I got something I want to show you."

"Is it important?" Mother would say, fatalistically putting aside her papers and starting to get up from her swivel chair.

"You know I wouldn't bother you if it wasn't important."

"Would you mind making a check on the interruptions chart?"

"Yes, Ma'am. The chart seems to be working fine, Mrs. Gilbreth. The children ain't bothering you half as much."

"The *children* seem to be getting the idea."

"I wisht you'd make one for the kitchen. They interrupt me all the time. I wisht someday you'd move your desk out there and see what I put up with."

Mother, rolling her eyes skyward for the benefit of Miss Butler, would follow him to the kitchen, to be shown a picture that Bob had drawn, a mole that Mr. Chairman had dug from the front lawn, or a new trick that Tom had taught the cat.

Meanwhile, we watched the mail anxiously for replies to Mother's prospectus. For almost two weeks, there was none. Then five arrived within two days—from the largest store in the world, in New York; from a drug manufacturer; a tool company; a dairy products distributor; an electrical appliances corporation.

There was a wait of another week, during which it seemed

certain that the course would have to be canceled. And then acceptances arrived from abroad—from a Japanese engineer, a Belgian technologist, and a representative of a British food concern.

That made eight, and when the tuition money was received, and deposited by Martha, the bank balance was enough to guarantee that the family could stay together for another twelve months, that Anne could finish Michigan the next year, and that Ernestine could enroll at Smith.

Mother planned, if possible, to run the course for five years, with a new group of students each year. By that time, Anne and Ernestine would have their diplomas, and Martha and Frank would be in college. That would mean only seven children to look out for at home, and Mother would be able to travel more, seeking consulting jobs. She hoped that in five years she'd be able to convince employers that she could work in a man's field.

On the night before the course opened, Mother told us she was going to need our cooperation.

"I know you'll all keep out of the office and the laboratory," she said, "unless it's something very important. And I hope you'll welcome all eight pupils, and treat them like friends."

We said we didn't know about that "friends" business. We knew the school was necessary from a financial standpoint. Frankly, though, we weren't enthusiastic about a group of outsiders coming into the house and monopolizing Mother's time.

"They're probably old cranks who are going to complain they can't concentrate because of the noise," Frank said.

"No they're not," Mother insisted. "I've met them, and they're all as nice as can be. I think you children will be fond of them."

"I know those old ones," Martha nodded. "Dandruff on their

blue serge suits, and always trying to get you in a corner to tell you about your dimpled little knees."

"Old ones don't talk about dimpled knees," Ernestine said. "They still talk about your trim little ankles."

"They're not old," Mother smiled. "At least not very. One of them is a woman—Miss Lies. She's from Macy's."

"Probably with a silky black moustache and mannish tweeds," Ernestine hooted.

Tom also was not pleased about the outlook, especially when he found out that one of the group was an Englishman.

"As if I ain't got enough work already," he complained, and with a good deal of justification. "Just keep them out of my kitchen, that's all. Especially the Limey—and that goes for the Jap, too."

He fished in a drawer for a pencil and paper, and made a great show of inventorying his tools, so that he'd know if anything disappeared.

We hid on a landing half-way up the stairs, and watched Mother's pupils arrive. The first was Mr. Yoyogo, the Japanese engineer. Tom, dressed in a clean butcher's apron and his chef's cap, answered the bell and let him in.

"You must be Yoyo," Tom said sullenly, purposely dropping the "Mister," but inadvertently omitting the last syllable. "You can put your hat and coat in there," he pointed to a closet, "and then go in the office, there." He pointed again, and started to return to the kitchen.

"You must be Tom," Mr. Yoyogo said. "Mrs. Gilbreth told us all about you. She says you do the cooking, laundry, help with the shopping, and do most of the heavy work in the yard. You must know motion study yourself."

Tom turned around. "Let me take your hat and coat," he said.

"I'm going to have to watch your motions," Mr. Yoyogo

told him. "You must have what the Gilbreths call The One Best Way."

"I'll learn you what I can, Sir," said Tom, holding open the office door for him.

The other six men arrived together in a cab, and again Tom answered the door. They were all in their late twenties or early thirties, and two of them were tall, husky, and handsome.

"Good night, just look at that," Ernestine whispered delightedly, forgetting for the moment all about upper New York State. "I've already changed my mind about not wanting to be friends. Anne'll die when she hears what she's missing."

"They're not what I expected," Martha admitted. "They don't seem like the dandruff type."

The men were laughing at something, and acted noisy and boyish. They asked Tom how tricks were, and started to take off their coats. Tom took the wraps from the two tall ones, who he apparently had decided must be Americans, and hung them up. But he hesitated before accepting the coats and hats of the other four. When he saw he couldn't pick out the Englishman, he took the rest of the wraps. Tom always believed in knowing who his friends were, though, so before he departed again for the closet, he asked:

"Does any of you gentlemen want a cup of tea?"

Nobody did.

"How about a crumpet?"

Nobody wanted one of those either.

"If you're looking for the Limey," one of the two tall ones grinned, and it was apparent that Mother had given all the group a thorough briefing on what to expect, "I'm your man. If you bring my coat back, I'll hang it up myself."

"Never mind," Tom said grumpily, "this time."

There was one more pleasant surprise for us, and Tom seemed

to find it pleasant, too. Miss Lies turned out to be young, blonde, slim and stunning. The chef's hat toppled off as Tom bowed her gallantly into the office.

We had to hurry away to school, without meeting Mother's pupils, and got no more than a glimpse of them as they left the house late that afternoon. But the next day Mother said she was going to serve them tea and apple cake, and that if we rushed home from school we could join the party.

The boys arrived for the tea in their school clothes, but Ernestine and even Martha, who was beginning to use lemon peels on her freckles, put on their best things—dresses with low waists and skirts above the knees, high heels, and rolled silk stockings with clocks down the sides.

Mother introduced us. "This is Ernestine, my next-to-oldest; and Martha; and Frank, my oldest boy; and Bill."

She was interrupted by Tom.

"If you've got time to come back to the kitchen, I've got something important to show you, Ma'am," he told Mother.

"Can't it wait until after tea?"

"Well," said Tom, looking crushed, "I guess it could. It ain't nothing much."

"It isn't anything Mr. Chairman has dug up, is it? You know I don't like to look at those things."

"No, Ma'am. It ain't nothin' like that."

Tom departed, and Mother began to feel sorry for him.

"It's probably the cat then," she said. "I guess I'd better go see it, or he'll never forgive me." She got up from the sofa. "If you'll excuse me. . . ."

"We'll go with you, if it's all right," Miss Lies said. "I've been dying to see what he comes into the office to get you for."

"I'm sure Tom wouldn't mind," Mother agreed.

Everybody filed out to the kitchen, and Tom **was** delighted with the size of his audience.

"You know how the children is always stepping on Fourteen's tail by mistake when she's eating?" Tom asked. "Well, I been putting her milk on top of the ice box and feeding her there."

"That makes sense," Mother agreed doubtfully.

"I lifted her up there twicet, and then look what I learned her."

Tom opened the ice box door and leaned in, as if to get a bottle of milk. The cat, which had been watching him from under a table, jumped onto his back and then to the top of the ice box.

"Bravo," shouted Mr. Yoyogo, who thus became a member of Tom's Club for a thousand years and four days.

"Smartest cat I ever trained, bar none," Tom gloated, pouring Fourteen some milk and flicking her whiskers with his forefinger.

All of us thought it was a good trick, and told him so.

"Let's see will he do it for you, Mrs. Gilbreth?" Tom said. He lifted down the cat. "Just lean in the ice box like you was getting some milk."

Mother shivered. "I can't stand to have anything ticklish on my back—you children know that," she explained. "Just the thought of it gives me the creeps."

Mother's back was her Achilles' heel. Sometimes, to tease her, we'd sneak up behind her and play creep-mouse with our fingers along her backbone. She'd squeal like a little girl, and shudder.

Finally Mr. Yoyogo agreed to volunteer for the experiment, and Fourteen performed as advertised.

"Bar none!" Tom repeated. "She's the smartest."

"From now on," Miss Lies told Tom, "whenever you tell Mrs. Gilbreth to come back here, we're all coming. I wouldn't miss anything like this."

Miss Lies was in the Club for a thousand years and four days, too.

After we had returned to the parlor, Mr. Bruce, the handsome American who represented the drug firm, said he wanted to get all of us straight.

"I know the two biggest girls are Ernestine and Martha," he said. "Which is Ernestine?"

"I'm Ernestine," she told him, sending her eyelashes into a flutter designed to cause boys to leave home.

"And I'm Martha," cooed Martha, with a slow, open-lipped smile, also designed to lure striplings from their domiciles.

"You can tell them apart," Frank said, "because Martha has the dimpled knees, and Ernestine has the trim little ankles."

Mother said that would be sufficient from Frank, and the men replied they had seen nothing deficient in the knees or ankles of either girl. Somehow, though, they seemed more interested in Mother's apple cake and in the younger children, than in the high-school girls.

"I'll bet," Bill told Mr. Bruce, "that you used to play football when you were a boy."

"I used to play some," Mr. Bruce conceded. "But that was quite a while ago. Before the War. I don't believe I've touched a football since."

It developed that all the men had played football or rugby at one time or another, except Mr. Yoyogo, whose game was baseball.

"You boys don't happen to have a football, do you?" Mr. Bruce asked. "It might be fun, sometime, to get a little exercise by passing it around."

"Sure we do," Bill said. "We can pass it right now."

"Oh, not now," Mr. Bruce said hastily. "I just meant sometime. We're having tea now."

"Go ahead if you want to," Mother told him. "Miss Lies and the girls and I will chat. We won't be going back to work for a half hour or so."

"The men don't want to play games with you boys," said Ernestine. "Why don't you stop bothering them?"

The men didn't seem to think it was a bother. After asking Mother if she was sure she didn't mind, they followed the boys out to the side lawn, and picked sides for a game of touch football. All the men played except Mr. Yoyogo, who said he'd have to watch until he learned the rules.

Tom was cutting the grass up front, and walked over to join the Japanese on the side lines.

"You don't like exercise, Mr. Yoyo?" he asked.

"I like it. But I never played before."

"If you like exercise," said Tom, "I'm going to learn you some motion study about cutting grass."

They walked over to the lawn mower, and Tom explained that his method was to cut one row up, and then one row back, and then one row up again.

"Very ingenious," Mr. Yoyogo told him, with a straight face. "Now in Japan we never thought of that. We cut one row up, then carry the lawn mower on our shoulders back to where we started, and cut another row up."

"There's a lot of things I can learn you," Tom assured him. "Why don't you try it my way, and see how it works?"

The Japanese, who really did like exercise, started out with the lawn mower. Tom sat down on the grass, to give instruction in case Yoyo should get mixed up and hoist the lawn mower up on his shoulders.

Mother, Miss Lies, and the girls came out and sat in the hammocks on the side porch, where they could watch the football game. Mother held Jane on her lap, and darned socks. Miss Lies showed Ernestine and Martha a new way to roll up their hair.

Mr. Bruce called his team back into a huddle and explained that the next play would be a long pass to Bill, in the end zone. The Englishman, who was backing up the line of the opposing team, slapped his squatting lineman on the part of the anatomy that was nearest him, and urged them to fight fiercely. Tom was half asleep, dragging indolently on a cigarette, in the front yard. Mr. Yoyogo, having sheared the front grass to perfection, guided the lawn mower resolutely toward the back yard, where the grass was nearly six inches high.

Mother told us at supper, after her students had gone back to New York for the night, that they had agreed a little exercise period every day would be beneficial.

"I want to tell you how much I appreciate your being so cooperative," she said. "I know it's not easy to have strangers running around the house and yard."

"Aw, that's all right," Bill said.

"And I don't want you girls to think that you have to change your clothes every afternoon, or you boys to think you have to play football with them, if you don't want to."

"Will there be tea tomorrow?" Ernestine asked eagerly.

"A little after three o'clock," Mother nodded.

"We should be able to start the game by 3:30, at the latest," Frank said.

10

EFFICIENCY KITCHEN

MOTHER thought one way she might get motion study contracts was to apply time-saving methods to the kitchen. Manufacturers would listen to a woman, she believed, when the subject was home appliances.

If the only way to enter a man's field was through the kitchen door, that's the way she'd enter.

Her students helped her build an electric food mixer, and draw up blueprints for new types of electric stoves and refrigerators. Mother planned, on paper, an efficiency-type kitchenette of the kind used today in a good many apartments. Under her arrangement, a person could mix a cake, put it in the oven, and do the dishes, without taking more than a couple of dozen steps.

On the strength of her blueprints, she landed a contract with a New York electric concern. The fee was one Dad wouldn't have considered. But it was the first job Mother had got on her own, and she was proud of it.

Someone in the electric company told the newspapers about

the contract. A woman engineer with eleven children was considered good copy. And in 1924 the idea of a scientifically planned kitchen was news.

The company arranged a press conference for Mother in New York. The resulting stories, besides telling of Mother's plans, managed to give the impression that our kitchen in Montclair also was a model of efficiency.

Actually, the exact opposite was true. Our kitchen, the one Tom used, was a model of inefficiency. Not that there was a handpump over the sink or a spit to roast fowls on, but it was almost that bad.

Our house had been built when the stress was on spaciousness, and the original owner had planned the kitchen to accommodate three or four servants.

When Tom baked a cake, or baked what he said was a cake, he had to walk about half a mile.

The distance from the sink, which was at a back-breaking level, to the old-fashioned gas stove was a good twenty feet. The food was kept in a pantry twenty feet from the stove and forty from the sink. And the dishes were in a butler's pantry, about the same distance away but in the opposite direction.

The refrigerator was in an alcove by itself. To get to it, you had to detour around a stand holding the bird cage; around a table holding Tom's tools, a plumber's friend, western story magazines, and back copies of *The Newark Star-Eagle;* and usually around Mr. Chairman, or Fourteen, or both.

But on the strength of the write-ups about the contract, a newsreel man phoned Mother and said he'd like to bring a crew to Montclair to photograph her in her efficiency kitchen.

"I'd love to have you," Mother told him, "but you see we

haven't set up the efficiency kitchen yet. All we have are the blueprints."

"That's all right," the newsreel man said, "we'll just shoot you in your kitchen there at the house."

"I don't believe that would be exactly suitable," Mother gulped.

"The public would never know the difference. They don't know one efficiency kitchen from another."

"They don't?" Mother stalled.

"No. And I'm sure that, being an efficiency expert, the kitchen in your home must be pretty much the latest word."

"But what we want," said Mother, "is the very latest word, isn't it? Not just pretty much."

"What we really want, Mrs. Gilbreth, is just some human interest stuff. Nothing scientific. Just you in the kitchen with the children around."

"I see," Mother said brightly, groping desperately for a way out. "Human interest." She thought of Tom's kitchen. Now if what they wanted only were animal interest. . . .

"We can come out any day this week that's convenient."

"I'm afraid I'm all booked up this week. How about some other time?" Her tone of voice was meant to convey that some other time like the year after next would be just right.

"We want to get this while the story's still news. It'll be fine publicity for your business. And it will only take a few minutes."

"All right," Mother surrendered. "Let's make it Saturday, then. Say three o'clock Saturday afternoon."

The course wasn't in session on Saturdays and, more important still, Tom would be off duty. Both Dad and Mother had tried in the past to modernize the kitchen, but Tom and his predecessor had been set in their ways. Mother decided that the least said to Tom about the matter, the better.

She drew up a diagram for our kitchen, and she arranged with a plumber and a gas man to come Saturday to raise the sink and move the stove.

Tom usually left the house after lunch Saturdays, and returned early Sunday mornings. This time, Mother gave him the whole day off and he departed shortly after breakfast. He was in a gay, holiday mood. He intimated that a large segment of the female population of West Orange, a town bordering on Montclair where Tom spent most of his time off, was going to be in for a pleasant surprise when he made his appearance four hours ahead of schedule.

The plumber and gas man finished their work by noon. We carried Tom's tools and the reading material down into the cellar, and put the canaries in his room in the attic.

Then Mother made chalk marks on the floor, from her diagram, showing us where she wanted the refrigerator, the table, and a cabinet for food, pans, and mixing bowls. We moved them into place, gave the room a scrubbing, and set up a sort of breakfast nook in the unoccupied half of the kitchen, where the stove used to be.

Mother went through the motions of making an apple cake, in a dry run to familiarize herself with the location of everything. She scarcely had to move her feet at all. She could reach each appliance from a spot in the center.

Apple cake, incidentally, was the only dish whose ingredients Mother thoroughly understood. She had grown up in a home where a Chinese chef ruled the kitchen. And she hadn't had time, since her marriage, to learn much about cooking. But apple cake had been one of Dad's favorite dishes, and Mother had memorized the recipe and just how it went together, so she could fix him midnight snacks when he worked late.

Efficiency Kitchen

When the newsreel crew arrived, we were dressed in our best clothes—especially Ernestine and Martha, who weren't overlooking any bets in case Hollywood was hunting for new talent.

While the crew was setting up lights in the parlor, the man in charge explained what he wanted.

The idea was that Mother would be playing the piano, and we'd be grouped around singing. Mother would turn and ask a question, and we'd lick our lips and rub our stomachs. The scene then would shift to the kitchen, where Mother would be making something with a minimum of motions. And the finale would be in the parlor again, where we'd be eating what she had cooked.

"Is there something you can make that won't take too long?" he asked Mother.

"I think so," she said.

"How about chicken chop-suey?" asked Bill.

"Or blueberry pie?" said Frank.

"I don't believe there is a blueberry in the house," Mother smiled.

"There are apples, though," said Ernestine, coming to her rescue.

"Apples?" said Bill, as if he were reading a part in which he had been carefully coached. "That sounds simply capital."

"Bully," said Frank in the same tone of voice. "I have a suggestion to make, Mother. Why don't you make us an apple cake, for a change?"

"Cease and desist," Mother laughed. "The children are teasing me," she explained. "I'm really not much of a cook. Apple cake is about the extent of my repertoire."

The newsreel man said he was sure Mother was being too modest, and that apple cake would be splendid.

The scene in the parlor went fine. Of course the movies were silent, and everything was done in pantomime.

Then we adjourned to the kitchen, and the men were impressed with the arrangement of the appliances.

"I don't see why you hesitated a minute about having pictures made of this," the man in charge said. "Women are going to go crazy when they see this setup."

"Of course the stove isn't what it should be, and neither is the refrigerator," Mother explained. "I want a stove that stands up high, so you don't have to bend over to see what's in the oven. And I want a refrigerator that you don't have to lean into."

The lights were adjusted, and Mother stood in the center of the working space. She lighted the oven. She pared and cored the apples with a gadget Mr. Yoyogo had made for her. She mixed and sifted the dry ingredients, and she greased the pan. So far, not more than four or five steps. The camera ground away.

Then she opened the refrigerator door, leaned in, and picked up two eggs with one hand, and a bottle of milk with the other. Just as she started to bring them out, Fourteen appeared from under a table, and jumped. She landed on the small of Mother's back.

"Eyow," Mother screamed. She threw her hands up over her head, and scattered dairy products from the breakfast nook to the butler's pantry.

"Cut!" roared the head of the newsreel crew. "What in the devil goes on here?"

"Who did that?" Mother shouted accusingly to Frank and Bill. "It's all right to tease, but Mercy Maude!"

Fourteen strutted across the top of the refrigerator, obviously proud of herself. Mother looked at the cat as if trying to decide whether to wring her neck now, or wait until the company had gone.

"I'm sorry, boys," she said. "I should have known you wouldn't have done it, at a time like this."

We couldn't help but giggle. And the camera men, who had been trying not to laugh, exploded.

"Down, Fourteen," said Mother, still a little indignant and making an ineffectual swipe or two at the cat. "Down I say, Sir."

Fourteen who knew Mother well enough to be certain nothing would come from the swipes, continued strutting. Mother reached over the sink to the shelf where Tom kept his Quinine Remedy, and the cat jumped down and slunk out of the room.

Mother started chuckling herself, and then she had an awful thought. A few years before, a newsreel company had taken some pictures of us at the dinner table in Nantucket. When they were released they were preceded by a caption saying: "The family of Frank B. Gilbreth, time-saver, eats dinner." Then the action was projected at about ten times the normal speed, while the theater audiences howled.

"I want you to promise me," Mother said to the man in charge, "that you won't show the part with the cat."

"Good night, lady, I know you've got eleven mouths to feed," he protested. "I wouldn't do you like that."

He kept his word, too.

Ernestine and Martha mopped up the eggs and milk, and Mother started in again, at the point where she leaned into the refrigerator.

Tom picked that particular Saturday to return early from West Orange. It always made him nervous, anyway, to be away from the younger children for too long, since he was convinced no one else looked after them properly. He also was sure that, as soon as he left the house, we turned his room and kitchen upside down, looking for candy or for future surprises that he might have hidden from us. Having left home earlier than usual, he apparently had decided that he'd better get back earlier, too, and check up on us.

He came in the back door, just as Mother was putting her cake in the oven. His first glance at the rearranged kitchen confirmed everything he had suspected. He stood there glowering, until the final cut.

"Oh, good afternoon, Tom," Mother said guiltily as she stepped out of the work space.

"What's happened to my kitchen?" Tom demanded. "And who scared my cat so she won't come into the house?"

Mother wanted to get the cameramen out of there before Tom said any more about the kitchen being rearranged.

"If you gentlemen will just step into the parlor," she told them, trying to push them through the door.

"And where are my birds at?" asked Tom. "You know I can't do no cooking without my birds."

"I'll tell you about it later, Tom," Mother said firmly. "This way, gentlemen, if you please."

The cameramen, who were picking up their lights and other equipment, were frankly intrigued.

"This is Tom, our cook," Mother finally introduced him. "We couldn't get along without Tom, could we children?"

"You're going to have to get along without me," Tom sulked, "if someone don't help me move my stove and freeze box back acrost the room where they belong."

"All right, Tom," Mother gave in.

"I ain't going to work all hemmed up like that," Tom pouted, half apologetically. "I ain't no midget, you know."

11

LYNCHING PARTY

MOTHER'S course recessed for the Christmas holidays. Anne arrived home from college December 19, and Al Lynch came to visit Ernestine the following day.

Ernestine had spent the preceding month instructing us on how to behave in his presence.

No one was to start eating at mealtimes until everyone was served. Frank was not to forget to help Mother into her chair. Martha was to refrain from discussing the cost of various items on the menu. Mother was to be sure Bob and Jane didn't go around the house with their rompers unhinged. All of the boys were to give Al top priority in their bathroom.

"All I'm asking," Ern kept telling us, "is that for four days you try to make believe that we're reasonably civilized."

It seemed like a fair enough request. Our first impression of Al had not been favorable. But first impressions often are unreliable, and if Ernestine had her heart set on impressing him, we thought the least we could do was cooperate.

[115]

"We're going to try to make everything go smoothly," Mother promised her. "Now don't you worry, dear."

Frank and Bill moved out of their bedroom, and doubled up with Fred and Dan. Anne and Martha helped Ernestine change the sheets on one of the beds, clean the room, and stow away radio parts, arrowheads, hockey sticks, some things in glass jars containing formaldehyde, and other miscellanea. The girls also cleaned the parlor, since Ern planned a buffet supper so that her Montclair friends could meet Al.

We knew Al was driving down from college, and we expected he'd arrive in an old Model T, probably with writing on the body. We were sitting in the dining room, just finishing lunch, when a new, 1925 Packard roadster pulled into the driveway. There was no writing on it, except for the initials A.L., in six-inch letters on the doors. Behind the wheel, wearing the most luxurious raccoon coat we had ever seen, was Al.

"That coat," Martha whistled, "cost $600 if it cost a nickel. And goodness knows what a Packard costs."

"Don't you ask him what it cost, either!" Ernestine warned.

"You can count on me to act civilized," Frank told Ernestine. "If you can land him, none of us will ever have to work."

"Get away from those windows," begged Ernestine, who herself was peeking from behind a curtain. "Golly, look at that catsy car!"

"Everybody sit down," Mother ordered. "Where are your manners?"

We came back to the table and heard Tom go to answer the doorbell. A moment later he opened the door from the front hall into the dining room, and stuck in his head.

"It's for you, Princess," he announced. "And from the coat he's wearing, it's a good thing nobody ain't out hunting today in the royal woods."

"That will do, Tom," Mother said sternly.

"Henc, henc," Tom wheezed. "I seen him before at Nantucket."

Ernestine glared at him and put her forefinger to her lips, but tried to laugh gaily.

"When he came in," said Tom, "I ast him for six cans of peas. He jumped and said, 'Yes, sir, anything else?' Henc, henc."

"It's so amusing to have Tom around, don't you think?" Ernestine said loudly. "Will you be good enough to excuse me for a minute, Mother dear? I'll just run out and see who it is."

"Bring him right in," Mother told her. "Perhaps he'd like some dessert."

Ernestine walked to the dining-room door. "Why it's Al!" she exclaimed. "How delightful!"

She closed the door behind her, and we heard some running in the hall.

"I didn't know he came from a wealthy family," Anne whispered.

"He wrote Ern about it," Martha explained. "His father sold his produce business and bought some stocks."

Ern and Al appeared in the dining room with their arms around each other's waists. Al had hung up his raccoon coat and porkpie hat, and there was a ring around his patent-leather hair, where the hatband had rested.

"We'll leave your suitcases and ukulele in the hall," Ern told him. "I'll see that our man takes them up to the guest room." She glanced apprehensively toward the butler's pantry, but Tom was fortunately in the kitchen, out of earshot.

Just as at Nantucket, Al still seemed a little too collegiate. Only now he also seemed a little too opulent. His clothes were new, extreme, and expensive. His plus-eight knickers hung almost to his shoes, and a jeweled tie pin sparkled above the neck of his blue and white checked sweater.

Al was smiling, and very handsome. He considered himself well in command of the situation.

"Greetings and salutations, everybody," he said. "Just one great big happy family, eh?"

We said greetings and we guessed he was right. All the boys stood up—Ernestine had instructed them carefully on that.

"I'd like you to meet my mother," Ernestine said formally. "Mother, may I present Mr. Lynch."

"How do you do, Mr. Lynch," said Mother. "We've all been looking forward to your visit."

"Meased to pleet you," Al chuckled, wringing her hand. "Meased to pleet you. My friends call me Al."

"That's nice," Mother said, favoring him with what was meant to be a cordial smile. But she looked as if she wondered what his enemies called him; and as if, providing they were searching for a word, she might be able to supply it.

"And this is Anne," Ernestine said. "She's just home from Michigan."

"Press the flesh," said Al, pressing it. He didn't exactly go into a clog dance when he put out his hand. But you had the feeling that he might. "Where have you been all my life, baby?"

We thought Anne was going to tell him she had been hiding from him, but instead she swallowed and asked him how things were at Sagiwan Agricultural and Technical.

"Fine and dandy," Al boomed. "Couldn't be better. I guess you read about how we massacred the football team from Wallace Teachers?"

"Isn't that," Anne guessed, "the traditional Turkey Day classic?"

"It sure is," Al agreed. "You read about it, eh?"

"It was splashed all over the front pages of the papers out in Michigan," Anne said innocently. "I wish I had thought to save you the clippings."

Ernestine introduced him to the rest of us, and we all pressed the flesh. He pulled a chair up backwards to the table, and sat with his legs straddling the back.

"Did you pipe the chariot?" he asked Ern, pointing nonchalantly, hitch-hiker fashion, with his thumb toward the window.

"Why, no," said Ern. "Where is it?" she went to the window. "Gosh, is that yours? Why, isn't that a Packard?"

"A little something the old man gave me for Christmas. Cost more than two thousand beans."

"Does that answer your question?" Anne asked Martha.

"Isn't that grand," Ernestine exclaimed. But there seemed to be some doubt in her voice. Al in Montclair, with the family, didn't seem quite so attractive as he had when they were alone in Nantucket.

While he was eating the tapioca Mother served him, Al told us about how he had scored two touchdowns against Wallace Teachers; about how the old man was building a little twenty-room place, that would cost seventy-five thousand beans, on the Niagara River; about how the Tau Tau Taus had stolen a small structure from a farmer's backyard and had put it on the front porch of the Tri-Alph house, just before the guests arrived for the big annual homecoming swing-out.

We listened, even supplying the necessary polite laughter. But we knew now, if ever there had been any doubt, that he wasn't the man for Ernestine.

Al and Ern decided to go riding in the Packard after lunch. Al was buttoned up snugly in his fur coat, and Ern not so snugly in her wool one. It was below freezing, and Ern was a little worried about whether she'd be warm enough in the open car.

"It's all right, baby," Al assured her as they said good-by to us in the hall. "If you get cold I'll give you part of my coat—the sleeves."

He threw his arms around her, to demonstrate, and then turned her loose, roared, slapped his knee, and actually nudged Mother.

"I think, Ern," said Mother, wincing and looking as if she'd like to wrap Al's ukulele around his ears, "that you'd better run upstairs and get a blanket."

Ern went and got one, and then they were off to the tune of a horn that played the first bar of "Jingle Bells."

"You can see for yourself she's made a terrible mistake," Martha told Mother indignantly. "You're going to have to tell her so."

"I don't think it's fair to judge the boy on such a short acquaintance," Mother said.

"We're trailing by one point," Frank mimicked, "and we're on the thirty-five-yard line."

"Thirty-five-yard stripe," Martha corrected.

"Stripe," Frank agreed. "I call the signal for a drop kick, and the center . . ."

"Pivot man," said Martha.

"And the pivot man looked back like he thought I was crazy. The stands are going wild."

"You stop that," said Mother. "He's Ernestine's friend and he's a guest, and that ought to be enough for all of us."

"It's certainly enough for me," Martha replied. "I'll bet two thousand beans on that!"

"Suppose he should become our brother," Fred said. "How would you like that, Dan?"

"A good question," Martha agreed. "Now go up and wash your mouth out with soap."

We thought Anne, as the oldest, should try to help us make Mother see the light. But Anne merely grinned knowingly at Mother, who tried to avoid her glance.

"We're not going to discuss the matter any more," Mother said. "I want you boys to take his suitcases upstairs, and I don't want anybody to do anything to hurt Ernestine's feelings."

Frank and Bill each took a sticker-spangled suitcase, and Fred followed with the ukulele.

"If Dad were here," Bill said as he deposited the bags at the foot of his bed, "he'd run that sheik out of the house and all the way over the state line."

"When he pulled that stuff about keeping her warm with his sleeves," Frank agreed, "that's when Dad would have swung at him. Mother doesn't understand what things like that can lead to, the way Dad did."

The boys decided that as the men of the house it was up to them to get rid of Al. Since it was futile to work on Ernestine, the best approach was to do a job on Al.

All the boys took baths that afternoon, and toward the end the hot water gave out. Frank got a screw driver and took the bolt off the boys' bathroom door. Bill opened the bathroom window.

In spite of their coats and the blanket, Ern and Al were blue when they returned home, about half an hour before the supper guests were to arrive. Both hurried upstairs to bathe and dress.

The boys were in Fred's and Dan's room, and they heard Al walking around as he unpacked and undressed. Finally they heard him enter the bathroom, experiment with the door to see why it wouldn't lock, and then slam down the window.

The water started to run in the tub.

"We'll wait about three minutes," Frank chuckled. "Can't you just see him now, shivering, leaning over, and running his finger under the faucet, waiting for the water to get hot?"

A chilled, unhappy baritone started to emerge from the boys' bathroom. Something about how undergraduates at Sagiwan were willing to give their all to the institution, and about how other seats of learning would find their lines riddled and their ends outflanked.

Mr. Lynch apparently was one who subscribed to the theory that if you couldn't lock it, the next best thing was to make such a racket that everybody would know it was occupied.

The water in the tub finally stopped running. The baritone became more chilled and unhappy, was choked off entirely in a shuddering gasp, and then was breathlessly resumed.

"He's under water," Frank said. "Go ahead, Bill."

Bill walked down the hall to the bathroom and went in. Al, sitting miserably in about an inch of water, grabbed for a washcloth when he heard the door open, and spread it over himself as best he could.

"Brrr," shivered Bill, "what have you got the room so cold for?"

"Good Lord," hissed Al, "I thought maybe you were one of the girls. For Pete's sake, close that door."

"Oh, don't worry about that," said Bill, closing it. "Nobody thinks anything about things like that in a large family."

"They don't?" Al asked dubiously.

"Nobody'll pay any attention to you if they walk in," Bill said. "They won't even notice you're in the tub."

"You mean they may come in?"

Bill shrugged his shoulders. "What have you got it so cold for? Is that part of the training rules?"

"I haven't got it cold on purpose, you can bet your sweet life on that," Al yelped. "The window was open, and there wasn't a drop of hot water."

"I believe I'd leave the door open," Bill suggested. "At least until the room warms up."

"Just leave the door closed. I don't come from a large family."

"Suit yourself, then. I'll ask Mother to heat some water on the stove and bring it up."

"Never mind," said Al, who wasn't sure whether Bill meant that he or Mother would deliver the water. "I won't be in here that long."

Bill helped himself to a glass of water and departed, forgetting to close the door.

"Close that door," Al hollered after him. "How many times do I have to tell you!"

"Okay," said Bill, returning. "Of course, if you *like* it cold in there." He slammed the door.

The older boys sent Fred and Dan together into the bathroom to wash their hands. Neither of them paid any attention to Al, who sat muttering in the tub, trying to finish his bath and get out.

Then it was Frank's turn. Frank had put on one of Martha's dresses, silk stockings, high heel shoes and a cloche hat.

"If he knows it's me," Frank said, getting cold feet, "he may get out of there and give me a licking."

"He hasn't been here long enough to tell any of us apart," Bill assured him. "And if we hear you holler, we'll all come running. We can handle him."

"Just to be safe," Frank insisted, "get the hockey sticks."

Frank entered the bathroom. As he heard the door open, Al made another precautionary grab for the washcloth.

"Yipe," he screamed, when he saw the female garb. He tried

to submerge all of himself under the surface of the water, but the one-inch level in the tub offered slight protection.

"Oh, hello there, Big Boy," said Frank, waving effeminately. "Did you have a nice ride? I'll only be a jiffy." He hurried to the sink and got a glass of water, drank it, and started out.

"Hey, wait a minute," Al growled. "I know you. You think you're pretty smart, don't you?" He made a grab, but Frank got by the tub, and out into the hall. Al didn't follow him.

Ernestine knew about there not being any hot water, because she had taken a bath herself. She was furious, but her guests started arriving and she had no chance to take the boys to task.

Ernestine answered the door and showed her friends into the parlor. There were about twenty of them. We knew them all, and liked them. We pulled back the rugs and started the phonograph.

Al was a little late coming downstairs. It may have been that he was hunched over a radiator, or it may have been that his wardrobe took a good while to adjust, or that he had to change his hair oil.

Ernestine's girl friends kept telling her they were dying to meet Al, and her boy friends said they wanted to meet the out-of-town sheik who had cut them out. None of them had failed to notice the Packard, parked out in front, and they were impressed.

Al finally made his entrance. All the other boys had on suits, but Al apparently preferred sweaters and plus-eights. He had his ukulele with him, and his life-of-the-party smile. He walked over and turned off the phonograph. Everybody stopped dancing, and he had the center of the stage.

"Greetings and salutations, guys and gals," he said, without waiting to be introduced. And this time he actually did do a clog step, ending up on one knee, like Al Jolson.

"A little number," said Ernestine's Al, "entitled 'I Used to Shower My Sweetie With Presents, But It Ain't Gonna Rain No More.'"

He threw back his head and started to strum the uke and to sing. "Dew ackker dew ackker dew, vo doe dee oh doe."

There was no doubt he could play the ukulele, all right. And his baritone was much better than in the icy bathtub. But you just couldn't start out a party that way, even in the Jazz Age. Maybe after midnight, after everybody had got to know him better, it might have gone over.

Ern's guests stood there woodenly, looking first at her and then at Mother, who was sitting near the fireplace with some knitting. No matter what Mother may have felt, she showed no disapproval.

Ernestine tried to help her beau. She started to Charleston alongside of him, and shouted "Come on everybody." She even licked first her right thumb and then her left, in a series of windmill gyrations known as pickin' cherries.

But it still didn't go over. And the worst of it was that everyone except Al realized exactly what Ern was doing and why she was doing it. They were pulling for her. Some of her girl friends started to Charleston alongside of her. And some of the boys began to sing along with Al.

"A little number," said Al, "entitled 'When Bathing Girls Take Up Aviation, I Want to Be There at the Takeoff.'" He laughed and strummed. You had to admit he was handsome. "Dew ackker dew ackker dew."

Ernestine was flushed and out of breath. She knew she couldn't stand another number, no matter how little.

"First Al," she begged, "please get up off your knees and let me introduce you."

Lynching Party

"I already introduced myself, baby," Al protested. He got up nevertheless.

"This is Mr. Lynch," Ern said, beginning to make the rounds. "He's visiting us for a few days, and we're having a peachy time."

"Meased to pleet you," grinned Al. He pressed the flesh.

Ern relieved him of his ukulele and put it on the back of the piano, where she hoped he wouldn't find it. Al drifted from group to group, listening to conversations about New York band leaders, Princeton and Dartmouth, new musical comedies, and happenings in Montclair. At first he tried to hold his own in the small talk, but no one seemed interested in hearing about the annual classic involving Wallace Teachers.

Even before supper was served, Al decided he had had enough of the party.

"Listen," he said, getting Ern into a corner, "get me out of here. Let's go for a ride or something."

"You know I can't leave now."

"What's the matter with your friends, anyway. Why don't they wake up?"

"Nothing's the matter with them," Ernestine said hotly. "It's you. You're acting like a fish out of water."

"I am eh? Well even a fish wouldn't dare go in the water around this house. In the first place, he'd freeze to death."

"I'm sorry about the hot water. But that's no excuse for you to act like you've been doing."

"And in the second place, a lot of wise guys would run him crazy parading around his goldfish bowl."

"What," said Ernestine, putting her hands belligerently on her hips, "do you mean by that crack?"

"I suppose you don't know your brothers keep parading in and out of the bathroom?"

"How would I know about that? And why didn't you lock the door?"

"And one of your brothers," said Al, ignoring the questions, "dressed up like a girl."

"No," moaned Ernestine. "Oh, no!" Then she started to giggle. "That must have been Frank or Bill. They're wise guys, all right."

"Just wait till I get my hands on them."

"It must have been kind of funny at that," Ernestine laughed, putting her hand on his arm. "Poor Al. What did you do?"

"It may seem like a joke to you," said Al, tilting up his nose, "but I found it typical of everything around here, including your friends."

"And how have you found everything around here?" Ernestine demanded.

"In bad taste. Extremely bad taste."

Considering the source, Ernestine thought that was one of the nicest compliments she had ever heard. She took off the Tau Tau Tau fraternity pin and handed it to him, and Al went up to get his bags. While he was upstairs, she took his ukulele from the back of the piano, and put it with his raccoon coat. Then she went in the darkened dining room, closed the door, and watched through a curtain as he got in his car and drove off to the tune of "Jingle Bells."

There wasn't much satisfaction, she thought, in the knowledge that time heals all wounds. If she could just be sure that time wounded all heels. . . .

After Al left, the party was a big success. One of Ern's friends from Dartmouth monopolized most of her evening. Everyone seemed to understand about Al. No one asked where he'd disappeared to.

12

ASH-TRAY CHRISTMAS

W̶E̶ DIDN'T have very much money to spend for Christmas, but it always was the most important day of the year in our house, and Mother intended to make it so again this year.

"I'd much rather have something you made especially for me, like a calendar or a desk blotter, than anything expensive from the store," she told us. "The best present of all is something given with love and affection."

We had been saving our allowances ever since summer, so there wasn't any real danger that we were going to have to rely exclusively on blotters and calendars. Also Ernestine and Martha now had lunch-time jobs as cashiers in the high-school cafeteria, and Frank and Bill had been doing yard work for neighbors.

A good many tree decorations from previous years were stored in the attic. But Mother knew there was happiness in anticipation of something pleasant, so she encouraged us to make fathom after fathom of paper chains from colored advertisements and illustrations that she'd clip out of magazines.

It was customary for each member of the family to give individual presents to all other members. But as fights and arguments occurred, the gift list of each of us seemed to become considerably shortened.

Almost every argument between Thanksgiving Day and Christmas ended with the announcement that the two participants were irrevocably severing Yuletide relations, and cutting each other off without so much as a blotter.

"Just for that," one participant would shout, "you're off my Christmas list forever. I'm taking the present I had for you right back to the store."

"I wasn't going to give you anything, anyway," the other participant would bellow. "Besides, that's the fourth time this week you've taken me off your list."

Of course all was forgotten and forgiven by Christmas. But if one had kept tabs, it would have appeared that only Mother was certain of getting presents from any of us.

In a good many families, the parents trim the tree on Christmas Eve, and surprise the children the next morning. Mother and Dad thought this was doing things in reverse—that the parents had both the fun of trimming and of watching the looks of pleased surprise. In our house, the children trimmed the tree, and the parents were surprised.

Mother was banned from the parlor on the day before Christmas. She wasn't even allowed to witness the arrival of the tree, which was brought home on Fred's express wagon and smuggled in through the kitchen door.

We trimmed the tree that night, while Mother worked alone in her office. We sang carols as we weaved on the tinsel and spread paper chains from the mantel to the chandelier.

Mother's office was separated from the parlor by a large sliding door, and sometimes we'd hear her soprano joining in. We seldom thought of Mother as being lonesome any more. But perhaps she was lonesome that Christmas Eve.

In a big family, the Santa Claus secret often leaks pretty far down the line. Not that anybody deliberately gives it away, but because too many lay it on too heavily for it to remain plausible. In our family, only Bob and Jane were believers, and even they were confused by the conflicting information heaped upon them.

Nevertheless, all of us hung up our stockings. After Bob and Jane went to bed, Mother filled our stockings and we filled hers. We carried our stockings to her, and then brought them back again when they were filled, since she wasn't allowed in the parlor.

With the bulging stockings hanging by the fireplace, we surveyed our night's work and found it good.

"The whole room," Jack sighed happily, "looks just like Woolworth's, only even better."

We usually had trouble going to sleep Christmas Eve. But once we dropped off we customarily slept soundly until about six o'clock, when Mother and the young children would rout the rest of us out of bed.

That Christmas Eve, Martha was restless and couldn't go to sleep at all. About two o'clock, she heard some tiptoeing on the stairs and a light click on. Martha waited a few minutes, and then put on a bathrobe and some slippers, and suspiciously tiptoed down, too.

The parlor door was open and the light was on. Sitting on the floor by the tree, with her back to the door, was Mother.

Martha saw her reach through the presents we had piled under the tree, select one, and then feel it, pinch it, rattle it, and smell it. Something must have told Mother she was being watched, because she finally looked stealthily over her shoulder and saw Martha.

Martha stood disapprovingly with hands on hips, and tapped her right foot on the floor. She didn't say anything.

"What are you doing up at this time of night?" Mother asked sternly, apparently deciding that a good offense was the best defense.

Martha shook her head and clicked her tongue.

"You should have been asleep hours ago," said Mother. "You'll be exhausted by dinner time."

"I'm going to tell on you," Martha informed her. "You're worse than Bob and Jane, aren't you?"

"I'd like to know what you mean by that," Mother protested. "Do you think that's any way to talk to your mother?"

"You can't be trusted a minute, can you? Just as soon as you think everyone's asleep, what do you do?"

"I investigate," said Mother, "to make sure everything is shipshape."

"What you mean is that you peek."

"A person with a naturally suspicious nature might put it that way," Mother admitted.

"You know you're not allowed in the parlor until we let you in. That's tradition."

"I know it," Mother giggled. "But your father and I always came down for a preview."

"You mean all those 'ohs' and 'ahs,' and the time Dad fell down in a dead faint, dazzled by all the brilliance, were just an act?"

"If you tell the others," Mother warned, "you may find ashes in your stocking."

"I always thought there was something funny about that fainting act."

Ash-Tray Christmas

"Up to the brim with ashes," Mother repeated.

"So all you want for Christmas," Martha said, "is a little love and affection. Well, you can't shake, pinch and smell those!"

"Sit down and have a pinch," Mother grinned. "I won't tell on you, if you don't tell on me."

"I'll be doggoned," said Martha, squatting next to her on the floor. "Do you see any for me?"

"Here's one to you from Anne," Mother replied, feeling, rattling, listening, smelling and using every other sense known to man—and some known only to women. "I think it's a pocketbook."

"You *think*," Martha scoffed. "You're as sure as if you had taken the package to the hospital and had it X-rayed."

We went down and got our stockings Christmas morning, and Mother took her first official look at the parlor. She didn't forget to "oh" and "ah," and to tell us that the tree never looked lovelier. We took the stockings upstairs to Mother's room, and opened them there. Then we cleaned up the wrappings, had breakfast, and walked to church. The air was bracing, and all of us felt happy and good.

Tom had a fire for us in the parlor when we returned. Mother sat down at the piano, and we went up to the second-story hall and formed a line by ages. Then Mother started to play *Adeste Fidelis*. We sang and marched single-file down the stairs and into the parlor. Anne led the way, as she always had done. In the past, Dad had brought up the rear, either carrying the baby or letting the baby stand on his shoes, while Dad took big steps and sometimes long jumps. This year Jane brought up the rear by herself.

We wound up the song standing around the piano, pushing

as close to Mother as we could. Frank did his best to sing bass, but all of us knew something was missing from the harmony.

Underneath the tree, besides the presents we had wrapped, were twenty or more cartons from relatives and friends. Mother slipped into the office to get a stenographer's pad and pencil, to make notes for the thank-you letters.

Frank started passing out the presents. The custom was that only one gift was opened at a time, so that everyone could watch and so that Christmas would last longer.

That year Dan had insisted that he was old enough to do his own Christmas shopping, and Mother had agreed. He had gone downtown by himself, pulling the express wagon after him, and had come home with the wagon piled high. No amount of pumping, even on the part of Fred from whom he had few secrets, could elicit the slightest information about the nature of the gifts.

It was obvious, though, from just a casual glance under the tree, that Dan's purchases were identical and that he had wrapped them without assistance.

There were eleven of them. He had placed them in a row, a little away from the general pile. Each was as large as a basket-ball, although irregular in shape.

Each gift, whatever it was, was enmeshed—trapped rather than wrapped—in green tissue paper, held in place with scores of stickers. Some of these wished you a joyous Yuletide; others voiced dire threats about what would happen if you opened it before Christmas.

All of us had wondered about Dan's presents, ever since he had brought them down from his bedroom the night before. Even Mother and Martha hadn't managed to pinch out a single clue.

In Christmases past, Dan had been primarily interested in

presents for himself. Sometimes he had been impatient at the delay involved in distributing the gifts one at a time, and had asked Dad to dig through the pile and find all of the presents for him.

But this Christmas Dan was quiet. Even when he opened a present for himself, he seemed detached and the usual enthusiasm was lacking. He kept his eyes on the eleven packages he had wrapped.

Mother sensed the situation and whispered something to Frank. Frank walked over to the row of misshaped green bundles and picked up one.

"To Mother with love from Dan," Frank read the scrawl on the tag. "Here you are, Mother."

Dan now was squirming with eagerness and embarrassment. "You probably won't like it," he mumbled. "It isn't much."

"I wonder what in the world it can be," said Mother.

"It's nice," Martha told her, dropping her voice, "that you have at least one surprise left."

"I can't imagine what it is, Dan," Mother said.

"Aw, I'll bet you've already guessed what it is," Dan replied. "It isn't much." His cheeks were flushed and he was staring at the floor. He knew all eyes were on him, and he didn't want to meet them.

Mother pulled off the last of the paper, and the thing stood naked and revealed.

To begin with, let us say it was a very big china ash tray, large enough to accommodate a whole family of chain smokers, which our family certainly was not.

Besides being large, it was hideous. It was, in fact, possibly one of the most hideous ash trays ever to come out of the Twentieth Century, which in future centuries may become best known for its production of the atomic bomb and hideous ash trays.

The main bowl was of white porcelain and looked as if it had no business being in the parlor. It was decorated with green and gilt cupids, nude except for floating pink ribbons that would have interested Isaac Newton. Around its perimeter were four holes, from which four unused cigarettes protruded. If one could forget the cupids, which one couldn't, the whole would have resembled the business portion of a cow, inverted and ready to milk.

A look of pained incredulity, that any such monstrosity could be devised by a fellow human being, passed briefly across Mother's face. For a moment she couldn't say anything.

"I guess you don't like it," said Dan, now looking straight at her. "It doesn't look like much, once you get it home from the store."

Mother tried to talk, but at first nothing came. Frank almost laughed, but Anne kicked him.

"I thought it was wrapped real nice, anyway," Dan said desperately, fighting off tears. "And the cupies are pretty, even if nobody smokes."

"Why Danny, dear," Mother whispered, now fully recovered, "it's just what I've always wanted. And just what we need around here, especially when there's company. Do you mean to tell me you picked this out all by yourself?"

She went over to him and kissed him.

"Aw," said Dan, and his eyes were aglow now, "it's not so much. Do you really like it?"

"Look at it, children," Mother told us. "Isn't it simply lovely? Such perfect taste. And so practical."

"It only cost fifteen cents, too," Dan crowed.

"Think of that, children," Mother said. "Only fifteen cents."

"The price is right," Martha conceded. "It's really beautiful, Dan."

"Some people have all the luck," Anne said, eying the ten similar packages. "I sure wish someone would give me something like that."

"Do you, honest?" asked Dan. "Honest?"

"Gosh, yes," said Anne.

"Gee, me too," said Frank.

"Same here," said Ernestine. "Lucky Mother!"

Frank went over to the row of presents and picked up another one. "To Fred with love from Dan," he read.

"Gee, give it here," said Fred, who knew a cue when he heard one. "I wonder what in the world it can be?"

Fred started to shred off the green paper. Dan relaxed and sighed. It was a sigh of ecstasy.

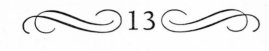

13

PLATFORM MANNERS

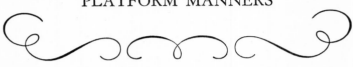

S OMEHOW Mother found the time to take part in Sunday school and Parent-Teacher affairs, to serve on the Montclair Library Board, and to make motion study speeches throughout the country.

Her platform manner was as natural as if she were talking to us in the parlor. Often she'd crochet or knit until she was introduced. She had a knack of popularizing a technical subject, by illustrating her points with everyday experiences. Her talks always went over well, and colleges and labor and management groups extended her an increasing number of invitations.

The money from the speeches didn't go toward running the house. Mother used it to set up special funds, so she could give us things that we wanted, but which the budget couldn't otherwise afford.

"The speech in Chicago will go for Martha's new overcoat," she'd say as she ran over her itinerary with us, "and the one in Detroit will be for Ernestine's college wardrobe."

Platform Manners

All of us wanted a small sailboat for Nantucket. Mother had Martha open a separate savings account at the bank—the Gilbreth Boat Fund. Certain speeches were earmarked for that account, and within two years it reached its quota.

Mother traveled by bus or upper berth, to keep her expenses down to a minimum. Most of the speeches were on week ends, so they didn't interfere with the course.

None of us liked her to be away from home. But we could see she was doing it for us, and it was easy to cooperate.

No fees, of course, were connected with the talks Mother made at our schools, and we thought that these were speeches she could well forego. In fact we would very much have preferred it, because they were a source of constant embarrassment. But we didn't want to hurt her feelings, so we didn't say anything about them at first.

Mother believed that every resident of a community had civic obligations and responsibilities. No matter how busy she was, she'd drop everything for a PTA meeting.

Her biggest school chore was the annual "Be Your Child" session. This was sponsored by the PTA, and the mothers were supposed to sit at their children's desks, meet their teachers, look over their textbooks, and review their papers.

The program was geared for mothers of average-sized families, and failed to take into account the unlikely possibility that someone might have eight children simultaneously in the school system.

Mother would hire a cab for the evening and race from home to the elementary school, where she'd sit at four different desks; from the elementary to the junior high, where she'd sit at two, and from the junior high to the high school, where she'd sit at two more. With the help of a memorandum book she managed to keep straight the compliments and complaints she received concerning each of us.

"I never thought I'd have to give an 'F' to one of your children," Frank's Latin teacher told her at one "Be Your Child" session. "I've had Anne, Ernestine, and Martha. But Frank is simply impossible."

"I know too much about what a fine teacher you are to believe you think any child is impossible," Mother replied with her sweetest smile. "Some pupils are just more of a challenge to teachers than others, isn't that right?"

"I guess so," the teacher said doubtfully. "Put it this way, then—he's the biggest challenge I've run into in fifteen years."

Mother made a memorandum to help Frank with his Latin, and to ask Ernestine to help him, too.

"I'll see that he's tutored at home, and I'm confident that meanwhile you'll work everything out," Mother challenged the Latin teacher, heading for the door and her waiting taxicab.

At the high school, Ernestine's English teacher was indignant. She had discovered that Ern had turned in a book report based—in fact lifted—from the blurb on the jacket, and hadn't bothered to read the book itself.

"I can't tell you how shocked I was, Mrs. Gilbreth. It's not at all the sort of thing Anne would have done. And I certainly didn't expect it from Ernestine. I always had considered her the soul of honor."

"I don't think there's really much reason to change your opinion," Mother replied a little hotly.

"I consider it plagiarism, plain and simple."

"Maybe it is," Mother said, "but thinking back I suppose I've done the same thing. Some times when I'm with a group of people who are talking about a new book, I guess I've given the impression that I've read the book, instead of reviews about it in the newspapers."

"Why I've done that too, I suppose, but . . ."

"It's really the same thing, isn't it?" Mother smiled.

"No, I don't consider it at all . . ."

"Don't reproach yourself for it," Mother interrupted. "After all, if a person tried to read everything that comes out, he wouldn't have time for anything else, would he?"

"I suppose not," said Ern's teacher, throwing in the sponge.

"There's no reason for you to feel bad about it. It's really laziness more than plagiarism. And all of us, whether we like to admit it or not, are a little lazy sometimes, aren't we?"

Mother headed for the door. But the fact she had dismissed the matter with such glib talk at school didn't mean she wasn't going to have a heart-to-heart talk with Ernestine.

Some of the teachers thought it simply impossible that Mother could earn a living and supervise us properly at home. Jack's kindergarten teacher, who was new to the school system, tried to pump him about it one day.

"What does your Mother do, John?" she asked.

"Lots of things," said Jack. "She's busy."

"Like what, dear?"

"She mends my stockings when there are holes in them, and serves the plates at the table, and gets me up in the morning, and tells me stories, and plays the piano so we can sing."

"But she can't do all that, John."

"Why can't she?" Jack asked suspiciously.

"Doesn't she have a career, John?"

"I don't think so."

"Why you know perfectly well she does," the teacher said accusingly.

"Well if she does," Jack shouted, "she never showed it to me."

When Mother started speaking to the Parent-Teacher groups, she explained about how she and Dad had tried to adapt motion study methods to bringing up a large family. This involved telling a number of stories about us, and we'd hear about them the next day from the children whose parents had been present.

That was bad enough. But when Mother was drafted for school assemblies and commencement exercises, it soon became too wet to plow.

Her first appearance was at Nishuane, the elementary school, where she told the children about how Dad had made motion studies of himself, so he could sleep later in the mornings. Dad used to lather his face with two shaving brushes, to save time, and could get into a tub, soap himself, rinse, and get out again, in a minute or less.

"It's a good thing to learn the quickest way to soap yourself," Mother said, "because then even if you oversleep you won't be late for school."

At recess later that morning, a boy in the sixth grade got a cake of soap from the lavatory, brought it out on the playground, and handed it to Fred.

"Here," the sixth grader said while a crowd quickly collected. "Show us how your father soaped himself."

Fred knew how, even though he was a half-hour soaker himself. But he had no intention of sitting down on the cinders and demonstrating, especially before a mixed audience.

"Come on inside," he mumbled, "and I'll show you there."

"No, right here," the big boy leered. "Here, take it and show everybody, so they won't be late to school." He cackled, and gave Fred a push.

Fred was in the third grade, and more than a head shorter than the other boy. It seemed hopeless to fight. If only Bill hadn't graduated up to junior high that year—when he was a sixth grader, Bill could handle anyone in Nishuane and frequently did, if sufficiently provoked. Fred took the soap in his right hand, and put it on his left shoulder.

"You start at this shoulder," he almost whispered, looking at his feet, "and you bring the soap down your left side."

A girl tittered, and Fred faltered.

"You bring the soap down your left . . ." Fred stopped, looked up from his feet, and drove soap and fist into the belly of his tormentor.

"See if you're big enough to make me do it," Fred hollered. Then, trying his best to imitate Tom's fighting stance and fierce grimaces, "I don't take nothing from nobody, understand? Nothing from nobody."

It felt good to be a man instead of a mouse, even if it meant a licking, and Fred grinned and walloped him again.

The sixth grader knocked him down, and sat on him. Fred was informed he either was going to eat the soap or go through the motions of lathering himself. About half the bar of soap had been forced down his mouth, before Lill, who was roller skating at the opposite side of the playground discovered what was going on and summoned Dan and Jack.

Lill went into action holding a roller skate by the strap and swinging it around her head. It wasn't exactly Marquis of Queensbury, but extraordinary action seemed called for. Dan used his fists and Jack kicked and bit.

A single blow of the skate took all of the fight out of Fred's antagonist, who quietly consumed the other half of the soap, while Lill sat on his forehead, Dan his feet, and Jack his stomach. Fred held his arms and did the feeding.

Lill and the boys wanted to tell Mother about it, so she'd stop making references to family incidents in any future speeches at their school. But the older ones talked them out of it.

"You'd only hurt Mother's feelings," Ernestine said. "What do they have, savages at your school?"

"They sure do," Fred agreed.

"The only reason Mother made the talk," Ernestine told them, "was because she thought she was helping you. And if you complain about it, she'll think you didn't appreciate it."

"If you want to know the truth," said Lill, "we didn't appreciate it very much. Everybody looks at you while she's speaking, and afterwards they giggle."

"And they feed you soap," Fred nodded. "The dark gray kind that's meant to take grease off your hands."

"The talk went over well, didn't it?" Ernestine asked. "You ought to be proud of Mother."

"It went over fine," Lill admitted. "We're proud of her. But I hope next time she gets asked to talk at your school."

Mother's next invitation was to address the junior high, where Frank and Bill were pupils. Frank told her at the dinner table, as tactfully as he could, that it would be a good idea to steer clear of family matters.

"Why of course I will, if that's what you boys want," Mother promised, but her feelings *were* a little hurt. "I won't make the talk at all, if you don't want me to."

"You ought to be ashamed of yourself," Ernestine told Frank. "Don't pay any attention to him, Mother."

"Oh, we want you to make the speech, don't we Bill?" Frank said with all the heartiness he could muster. "We're looking forward to it."

"Sure," Bill agreed, "especially if it isn't about the family."

Mother tried, in her speech at junior high, to explain the importance of standardizing nuts, bolts and machine parts, to eliminate waste. She saw she had aimed over the children's heads, so she sought to illustrate.

[144]

"Here's what I mean," she said. "Take boys' shirts. Almost every shirt has a different type button. When one comes off and gets lost, you know how much trouble your mothers have to find one just like it."

The children seemed to understand that, so Mother continued.

"Think how much time would be saved if all shirts had exactly the same kind of buttons. Do you know what I do? When one of the buttons comes off a shirt, I cut off the button at the collar, and move it down to replace the missing button. Then I just put any old button at the collar, because the tie hides it and it doesn't show."

Frank and Bill exchanged glances across the assembly hall; they knew that that had done it.

Three boys cornered Bill after school and demanded that he loosen his tie, so they could examine the button. Bill wouldn't have objected to showing them, if they had asked nicely. Bill was good-natured enough, but it usually was a good idea to ask him nicely.

In junior high school there were accepted rules about fair fights, so Bill could take on his opponents one at a time, and Frank's assistance wasn't needed. When it was over, Bill's tie was tattered and blood-spangled, but still proudly waved.

Ernestine and Martha once again persuaded the younger ones not to tell Mother what had precipitated the fight.

And then an invitation came through from high school, and the older girls were panic-stricken.

"We're ruined," Martha groaned.

"Thinking it over," Ernestine said to Bill and Fred, "giving the matter mature deliberation, I believe you two boys had better tell Mother what happened after she spoke at your schools."

"Tell her nothing," Bill grinned. "I enjoyed it. Anyway, we don't want to hurt her feelings."

"I don't see what you're scared of," Fred said. "They don't make you eat soap in high school, do they?"

"If you tell her now, after making us keep quiet," Bill threatened, "I'll give her some stories to put in her speech. Like about the time something fell off and tripped you when you walked into the movies, because you had used motion study by fastening it with a safety pin."

"Good night," Ernestine blanched. "You don't think she'd tell that one, do you?"

"Just don't go hurting her feelings," Bill warned.

Mother spoke at high school about process charts for industry. And she illustrated what process charts were by explaining about the ones we had in our bathrooms.

Few speakers ever got a better reception at the high school assembly. But Ernestine and Martha wished she'd take up bridge, like other mothers, or confine her speeches to audiences west of the Mississippi.

"You've got to be more careful," Martha stormed to Mother that night.

"It's gone too far," Ernestine agreed. "We'll never live it down."

"For goodness' sake, what's the trouble?" Mother asked. The girls seldom addressed her that way, and she was frankly concerned.

"It was bad enough when Fred had to eat soap—dark gray soap," Martha said. "And it was bad enough when Bill had to fight to save his necktie."

"But do you know what I've been getting all day?" Ernestine asked. " 'My, you look fresh as a daisy, baby. I'll bet you made a little mark on the bath chart before you came to school this morning.' "

Mother had had her usual full day. After her speech, she had come home and taught her course. There had been the customary interruptions by Tom. Dan was in bed with a sore throat, and she had spent half an hour reading to him, and another half hour playing Parchesi. The mending seemed to gain on her, no matter how much time she devoted to it. All in all, she was thoroughly tired and discouraged.

"I guess I put my foot in it," she agreed. "The only reason I made the talks was because I thought you children wanted me to."

"Well, gee, we did," said Martha, "only . . ."

"I try," said Mother, and there was no theatrics in it; just a statement of fact, "to do the best I can."

"We know you do," Ernestine told her. "We shouldn't have said anything about it."

"Why did Fred have to eat soap?"

"The story about taking a bath by motion study," Martha said.

"And Bill?"

"Buttons," said Ernestine.

Mother started out of the room. She was pale and her shoulders were sagging. Her red hair had begun to show traces of gray in the last few months. She looked defeated, and almost old.

"The talk went over swell, though," Martha said, running after her. "It was just that one little story."

"I never heard so much applause after a speech at assembly," Ernestine said, running too.

"You didn't?" asked Mother.

"You brought down the house," Martha told her. "We sure were proud of you."

"I'm glad you were, dear," Mother said, squaring her shoulders. "To tell you the truth, I thought it went over pretty well, too."

"You had them eating out of your hand," Ernestine nodded.

"I tell you what," Mother said, "I promise I won't accept any more invitations from the Montclair schools."

"Oh, we like you to speak," Ernestine said. "It impresses the teachers, and the kids, too."

"But no more stories about the family, is that it?" Mother smiled. "All right, I promise that, then."

"Just try to be careful," Martha begged, "not to say anything we wouldn't say."

14

MOTHER'S NEW NOSE

MOTHER left the house in a taxi one night that spring to speak at an engineering meeting in Jersey City. An hour and a half later, the chairman of the meeting telephoned us to see if Mother had been detained. The audience had been waiting twenty minutes, and she still hadn't appeared.

Our house was only eleven or twelve miles from Jersey City, and Mother as usual had allowed more than ample time for the trip. It wasn't like her to be late for anything. Perhaps the cab had broken down.

About ten o'clock that night, the telephone rang again. Ernestine answered it, and heard Mother's voice.

"For goodness' sake, where are you?" Ern asked her. "We've been worried to death. They called from Jersey City."

"I just telephoned them," Mother said, and her voice sounded muffled. "It's all right. There's nothing to worry about."

"Where are you now?"

"I had a little trouble, dear," Mother said. "And what do you think? I'm going to have a new nose."

The strain, Ernestine thought, has been too great for her. Something like this was bound to come. No woman could possibly raise a family of eleven, run a business, and make two or three speeches a week, without an eventual mental crack-up.

"Of course you are," Ernestine humored her. "And you've worked hard for it, too. You certainly deserve it."

"The new nose is going to look much better," Mother said.

"Oh, much," Ernestine agreed. "I'm sure of that."

"You know how thin the old one was—I never did like it. My father used to tease me about it, because it was just like his. His was thin, too, remember?"

"I'll see that no one teases you about it any more," Ern promised. "What you need is a nice, long rest."

"That's what the doctor says," Mother agreed brightly.

"Now you just tell me where you are, and I'll come and get you."

"I thought I told you. I'm right here in Montclair. They brought me to Mountainside Hospital."

Ernestine was sure then that the worst had happened. "You stay right there," she choked. "They give you the nicest noses there of any place I know."

"I'm looking through a magazine now to find just the kind I want."

"That makes sense," said Ernestine.

"They won't let anyone see me until tomorrow. I had a terrible time even getting them to let me use the phone. I'll have my new nose by tomorrow."

Then Mother explained from the beginning. Another car had run into the taxi and turned it over. Something had happened to her nose and right knee. A bone surgeon was coming

out from New York in a few hours to set the nose. They had
injected something into her arm at the hospital that had stopped
the pain and made her feel wonderful.

"There isn't much left of the old nose, I'm afraid," Mother
added, "so it's just as easy to give me a handsome one as the one
I used to have. Goodness knows nobody would deliberately
choose a nose like my old one."

Mother hung up, and Ernestine explained about the accident
to those of us who were still awake. Then she called the hospital
desk for additional details. Mrs. Gilbreth's condition was satisfactory, but painful. Visiting hours started at ten o'clock in the
morning. Children under twelve weren't allowed to visit.

All of us stayed out of school the next morning. We were sure
that, regardless of age rules, Mother would want to see everybody. In fact we were convinced that if she were deprived of
that privilege, her recovery would be seriously retarded.

Ernestine suggested that it might also cheer up Mother if we
took her some flowers from the yard. Lilacs, lilies-of-the-valley,
and daffodils were abundant, and the boys went out to pick
them. They wanted to cheer up Mother as much as possible, so
they systematically stripped the yard. When they were through,
the porch stairs were heaped with blooms and the lilac bushes
were reduced to squat shrubs.

Everyone's arms were full as we walked to the hospital, and
we had to stop and rest on several occasions. There was more
than the usual trouble filing across street intersections, because
it was hard to see through our bulging bouquets. Ernestine, in
addition to her bouquet, carried a suitcase containing clothes,
books, the morning mail, and some office work for Mother.

When we arrived at Mountainside, Ernestine, Martha, and
Frank went in and got Mother's room number from the desk.
Then Frank came out and brought the younger children in the

back way, through an emergency door used by the ambulance patients. Mr. Chairman came too, although he knew he wasn't supposed to, stealthily bringing up the rear of the line on his stomach. Dan discovered him in time, and everyone waited while Dan chased him out the door.

Single file, then, they tiptoed up the back stairs and along Mother's corridor, peering anxiously around corners to avoid doctors and the floor superintendent. Ernestine and Martha, who had gone up by the elevator, were standing outside Mother's room and gave the signal that the coast was clear.

Ernestine entered the room. The rest of us stayed in the hall. The bottom part of Mother's face was covered with bandages, and there was a cast on her knee. But she was sitting up in bed, knitting and reading a magazine. She was in a semi-private room, with two other patients. As it turned out, the man who collided with the taxi was required to pay the hospital expenses. But Mother wasn't taking any chances, in case we had to foot the bill.

"There you are," Mother sighed. "It seemed as if visiting hours would never begin. How is everything at home?"

"Oh, Mother," Ern called, running to her bed. "Does it hurt much? Are you all right?"

"Of course I am, and I'm getting a real rest. Sit down and let me look at you."

Mother introduced Ern to the other two patients, and Ern pulled up a chair. Mother kept glancing at the door.

"I don't suppose," she said, "that Martha or Frank came with you, did they? No, of course not. I forgot. Everybody'd be at school, wouldn't they? I know they have rules about the younger ones, but do you guess the others will come this afternoon?"

The rest of us came in then and piled the flowers around Mother's bed. Bob and Jane started to cry when they saw the bandages. They climbed on her bed and snuggled up against her.

"What's that for?" Mother said, kissing her hand through her bandages and placing it on each of their cheeks. "Why are you crying? Don't tell me you're jealous because I'm going to have the best-looking nose in Montclair."

Bob said he had liked the old nose, just as it was.

"That skinny old thing?" Mother said scornfully. "Huh!"

"Does it hurt?" we asked. "You can't fool us. Does it hurt much, Mother?"

"You can't get a handsome nose without having it hurt a little," Mother admitted. "But it will be worth it. You just wait for the unveiling."

She said that just seeing us and smelling the flowers had made her feel better, but that she was afraid the hospital officials wouldn't like it if they found we had broken the rule about children under twelve.

"I'd like to know how babies get born here then," Lill said. "They're under twelve."

"And another thing," Mother told us, "you mustn't miss any more school on my account. I want you to promise me that."

We promised. Ernestine said we'd all go to school that morning, just as soon as we left the hospital.

"We'll need written excuses for being late," Ernestine added. "I wrote them this morning. They're in the suitcase. All you'll have to do is sign them."

Ernestine dug in the suitcase and produced a typewritten original and seven onion-skin carbons. Mother glanced them over and signed them.

"Thank you, dear," she told Ern gratefully. "You write the nicest excuses in the family."

A nurse came in then, but she seemed more concerned about

the flowers than about our breaking the rule for children under twelve.

"I don't believe we have vases enough for all of them," she said, "and they can't stay there. Your Mother looks as if she's lying in a bier."

We hadn't realized it before, but that's exactly how it did look. The lilacs, lilies-of-the-valley, and daffodils were piled on both sides of the bed, as high as Mother herself. The nurse cleared a passage to the bed, and lifted off Bob and Jane.

"You mustn't get on the bed," she warned them. "You jiggle it, and your Mother's in considerable pain."

"Not any more, I'm not," Mother said.

"They say at the desk," the nurse told us, "that you children can only stay five minutes more, and for you to go out the back way, the same way you came in. They don't want people in the reception rooms to know that the rules have been broken."

"Everybody in the hospital has been so nice," Mother said.

"And use the back door again," the nurse continued, "when you come tomorrow—*after school.*"

15

CRAZY OVER HORSES

WE THOUGHT it would be a
good idea to surprise Mother by planting a vegetable garden in
the back yard. If we could grow some of our own food, it would
cut expenses considerably.

Ernestine had written the Department of Agriculture for instructions, and they came while Mother was in the hospital.
Martha went downtown and bought the seeds. Even Tom,
who was a city man and didn't realize how much work would
be involved, was enthusiastic.

We spaded up almost half an acre, raked it carefully, and put
in the seeds. We were worn out toward the end of the job,
which took the better part of two days, and Tom had to finish
most of the heavy work.

The soil was fairly good, but the Department of Agriculture
bulletins were unanimous in agreeing that fertilizer should be
added for best results. When Martha telephoned the seed store
to price fertilizer, she was appalled by the cost. She broke the

Belles on Their Toes

news to us out in the garden, where Tom was watering and the rest of us were surveying our work and digging up an occasional seed to see if it had begun to sprout.

"It'd cost $10—maybe more—to do the job right," Martha said gloomily. "We want to surprise Mother, but not with any bill for $10."

Tom's hands were blistered and his back was stiff. His original enthusiasm had waned, but he was determined that his work wasn't going to be wasted.

"You should of thought about the $10 before you half kilt me," he told Martha angrily. "Whatever it is, we want best results."

"It's fertilizer," Martha explained. "They want $10 for the commercial kind and $12 for manure."

"They want $12 for *that?*" Tom shouted. "Are they crazy? Don't let them cheat you!"

"That's what I told them," Martha agreed. "I told them not to think I was born yesterday."

"I'll get you all of that stuff you want," Tom promised. "And it ain't going to cost you a cent."

Martha said that was grand, but Ernestine wasn't sure Mother would approve.

"We don't want you to spend your money for it," she told Tom. "Maybe we can get along just as well without it."

"Don't worry about me, Doochess," Tom cackled. "I wasn't born yesterday, neither. But I got friends and I know where to get it wholesale."

Later that afternoon, he nailed a wooden box onto the express wagon, got three snow shovels out of the garage, and summoned Frank and Bill. They went out the back way, so the girls wouldn't see them, and started to tour the neighborhood. Milk and ice still were delivered from horse-drawn wagons, and some of the streets near our house were used as bridle paths.

No sparrow ever swooped down on what the trio was looking for, with more delight than did Tom.

"Henc, henc," he snorted while he shoveled. "I got friends all right. Some of my best friends is horses."

"Twelve dollars!" Frank said scornfully. "We ought to go into the business."

"I never thought I'd live to see the day when they sold it for money," Tom nodded. "Pull the wagon over closer, Billy. My back is broke from that hoeing."

The neighborhood was a fashionable one, and most of the residents knew us or Mother. Some of them waved from porches or opened windows, as Tom and the two boys paraded along the street with shovels on their shoulders and eyes optimistically peeled on the roadway.

A few chauffeurs wandered down their driveways for a closer look, but they were fortunately aware of Tom's reputation for belligerence, and they avoided trouble. None of them said any more than hello.

Tom seemed disappointed that he had no hecklers.

"Go ahead," he taunted one chauffeur, who must have been thirty years younger and eighty pounds heavier than he. "Why don't you ast me what we're doing?"

"Take it easy, Tom," the chauffeur humored him. "You're too tough for me. I'm not opening my mouth."

"You'd better not, neither," said Tom, looking significantly into the cart. "When I got through with you, you wouldn't dast to close it."

It took a couple of hours to fill the box. Tom and the boys brought the wagon home and dumped it behind the back fence, where the pile was out of sight.

"We'll go out every afternoon," Tom told Frank and Bill,

"as long as you behave yourself. If you ain't good, I'm going to leave you home."

The two boys, who had enjoyed themselves as much as Tom, promised they'd be good.

"Don't say nothing to the girls," Tom warned. "I think Martha would take it all right. But the Doochess would say it hurt her social standin'."

The boys got home in the afternoons ahead of the high school girls, and thus could get away without being noticed. It took a good deal longer the second day to fill the box, because they were covering the same territory. On subsequent days, they were forced to go farther and farther away from home. But the pile behind the fence grew steadily. And even after they knew the pile was high enough, they found excuses to go after more.

"We might need some for next year," Tom pointed out. "And every year there is fewer horses."

They soon found out which were the most productive streets, and how many days they should allow to elapse before going back over a street. Sometimes there'd be an argument about whether it would pay to go around a certain block, and the person who had advocated the detour would either crow or eat crow, depending on the pickings.

"Maybe we did go up there yesterday," Tom would say. "But I see sparrers. And where sparrers is, is what we're looking for."

Tom was invariably right in selecting the streets. He may have had some sort of sixth sense. Or, as Frank and Bill suspected, he may have cased the neighborhood during the morning, while they were in school, so as to impress them with his infallibility. At any rate, he swore he saw birds when neither of them did, and he could predict with exactness what would be found around a curve in the street.

Crazy Over Horses

The sport—because that's what they considered it—might have continued for weeks, if they hadn't bumped into Ernestine. They had carefully avoided the streets she and Martha took coming home from school. But on that particular afternoon, Ernestine had been given a ride part of the way home, and was off her accustomed path. She was walking with a fellow.

The boys and Tom didn't see her approaching. Bill had maneuvered the express wagon into position, and Tom and Frank were shoveling.

"Henc, henc," Tom was chuckling. "I tole you I seen sparrers. You can't fool old eagle eye. This is always a good place. This is an every day street from now on."

"That's eleven for Tom, and only five for us," Bill said enviously. "He can spot it a mile away."

"I'm the champeen," Tom crowed. "Ain't no doubt about that. It's the biggest one today, too. Those little ones of yours we might as well of throwed back."

He looked up then and saw Ernestine.

"Duck," he warned, squatting behind the cart, "or she'll have us beheadet when she gets us back to the palace."

Ernestine's friend was intent in a conversation. Frank and Bill had never seen him before, and he wasn't paying any attention to them. Ernestine had seen them and was watching them out of the corner of her eye. She was blushing and furious. She held her head high, and she tried to make believe she was listening to every word of the conversation.

Frank and Bill turned their backs, because they didn't want to embarrass her any more than they already had. Tom, peeking guiltily from behind the cart, started mumbling about how the robbers at the seed store wanted to charge $12.

Ernestine passed, without her friend's being aware that she

[159]

knew them. But as she walked down the street, she didn't feel right about it. No matter what they were doing, they were kith and kin. It was a cheap thing to pretend not to know them. And, after all, they were out collecting what they were collecting to save the family money.

"Just a second," she told her friend. "Wait up."

She turned and walked back to the wagon, and looked into it.

"Hello, Frank," she said loudly. "Hello, Bill. Hello, Tom."

They said hello, Ernestine.

"That's a fine load," she told them. "I think you'd better take it home, now."

They said they were glad she liked it, and that they were headed home.

Ernestine rejoined her friend, who hadn't seemed to be paying much attention.

"They're my brothers," she said defensively. "At least the two boys are. We're going to have a vegetable garden."

"That stuff will make it grow," he nodded. "We use it on **our** lawn."

"It sure will," Ernestine agreed.

"It's much better than the commercial kind."

"It sure is," she nodded.

"You might tell them we passed some of it back there a ways. Didn't you notice?"

"I don't think so," said Ernestine. "Anyway, they've got plenty of it already."

"It seems a shame to miss it. It gets more expensive every year."

Ernestine and her friend continued down the street. She wondered how romance was supposed to flourish for any member of a family with so many younger brothers. She wondered why,

with all the topics of conversation in the world to choose **from,**
they had to end up on that one.

Before Mother came home from the hospital, Ernestine
warned the boys not to mention how they got the fertilizer.
She thought Mother had enough on her mind without worrying about the fact that almost every one of her friends in town
must have seen Frank and Bill making the rounds with their
cart.

But the soil did look fine and rich, and it was one of the first
things Mother noticed.

"Where in the world did you get that lovely fertilizer?" she
asked. "I didn't see any check stub made out for that."

"It's a long story," said Ernestine. "It seems that Tom has **cer-**
tain friends."

"I guess you'd better not tell me," Mother smiled. "I have an
idea it's one of those things that the less I know about, the better
I'll feel."

"Have you ever heard of Pegasus?" Ernestine asked brightly.
"Well, once upon a time . . ."

"Never mind, dear," Mother interrupted. "I saw the box **on**
the express wagon."

"It won't happen again," Ernestine promised. "And you
ought to see all that's left over, out by the back fence."

Mother thought the garden was a wonderful idea. The seeds
started to come up before long. The jobs of weeding and culti-
vating were added by Ernestine and Martha to our work assign-
ment charts, and we were fairly faithful about them.

We may not have got best results because, as the agriculture
bulletins pointed out, manure is supposed to be aged before it
is applied as fertilizer. But we did, at least, get good results.
There were corn, beans, peas, carrots, tomatoes, beets, kale,

and lettuce. The girls canned some of them for winter use.

Later we got a dozen hens, and that cut expenses some more, and helped solve the fertilization problem for future years. Fred and Dan thought it would solve the problem altogether if we should buy a pony, but the older ones reluctantly vetoed that idea.

Tom named and made pets of the hens, and they'd follow him around the yard and jump up and perch on his finger. When their laying lagged, he'd make a show of spiking their mash with Quinine Remedy. The results after such dosings were spectacular. The poultry bulletins, which we also had written for, said the most you could expect from a dozen hens was eight or ten eggs a day. Sometimes we'd find twenty-five or thirty eggs in the nests when we got home from school.

Sometimes, too, we'd see empty, store-bought egg containers poking out from under old newspapers in the kitchen waste-basket. We didn't want to spoil Tom's joke. When he wasn't looking, we pushed them down out of sight.

16

THEN THERE WERE TEN

ANNE fell in love with a doctor at the University of Michigan, and this time it was the real thing. She wrote Mother that she had an engagement ring, and that her fiancé expected to go into practice soon. He was a few years older than she. He had to work pretty hard, and she didn't have a chance to see as much of him as either of them would like.

Anne didn't say so, but she wasn't interested in college any more. She was interested only in getting married. But she felt she had obligations to the family, and she didn't want to do anything that would upset Mother.

She was moody and nervous when she returned home for spring vacation. She spent a good deal of time in her room, writing special delivery letters. And she didn't look up any of her friends in Montclair.

Mother's nose had turned out as handsomely as she had predicted, and she was back, full-time, on the grindstone again. But now she was concerned about Anne, who didn't seem to want to confide in anyone.

Then There Were Ten

"I know what it's like," Mother said one night, dropping down beside Anne on her bed. "Goodness knows I went through the same thing when I was engaged to your father. I was in California and he was 3,000 miles away in Boston."

"No one knows what it's like," Anne said hopelessly. "Nothing was keeping you from getting married."

"Well, I was some older than you," Mother admitted. "I had already graduated from college. But you've only got a little more than a year to go."

"We'd like to get married right away," Anne whispered. She threw her arms around Mother. "Oh, Mother, what am I going to do?"

"It'll work out all right," Mother promised.

"It sounds selfish, I know that," Anne said. "But that's what we'd like—to get married right away."

"It doesn't sound selfish at all," Mother told her. "It sounds like the most natural thing in the world. If you didn't feel that way, I'd know you'd picked the wrong man. But I think it would be better for you to wait a while, dear."

"I know it," Anne burst into tears. "I know you'll need me here to help run the house until the younger children are grown."

"Lie down, dear, and let me rub your back."

"I know it, and he knows it," Anne sobbed. "We know it's out of the question."

"Why the children won't be grown for fifteen years," Mother said. "You don't think I mean for you to wait that long! I don't need you to help run the house. I just want you to wait until you finish college."

"But it wouldn't be right. It wouldn't be."

"Of course it would be right. Ernestine helps run the house now, just as well as you used to. And Martha will do just as well as either of you—even better, I suspect—when Ernestine goes off to Smith this autumn."

"Go ahead and rub," said Anne, lying on her stomach and drying her eyes on the pillowcase.

"You don't think I want a bunch of spinsters around the house, scolding me because the dusting isn't done properly, do you?" Mother asked, rubbing.

"You really don't?"

"And you don't think I want to support you forever, do you?" Mother teased.

"Well, naturally, I thought you'd want me to get a job."

"If you had a job, you wouldn't be any help running the house," said Mother, emphasizing her logic by slapping her where she sat down. "Why I'll be tickled to death to get rid of you."

"I wouldn't blame you if you were," Anne sighed. "I honestly wouldn't."

"But I do think it would be best to wait until you graduate. Just to set an example to the other children, for one thing."

Anne said that waiting a year wouldn't be anything. It was waiting fifteen, that had her worried.

"I wouldn't even ask you to wait that long, but you know how much your father wanted all of you to finish college," Mother explained, "I guess it's something I promised myself I'd do for him."

"And you're sure you're not going to need me at home?"

"It's a mistake ever to think of yourself as indispensable," said Mother, rubbing, and then slapping her in the same place again. "Why don't you telephone him and ask him if he can't spend the rest of the holidays with us. We'd all like to meet him."

Anne leaped from the bed. "I sure will," she shouted. "Why he'll pack up in a minute and . . . Wait a minute. You're not trying to give him the Al Lynch treatment, are you?" she asked suspiciously.

"Not unless he brings a ukulele."

"He's not like that. You'll see."

We called him Doctor Bob, to distinguish him from our own Bob. We couldn't decide whether we liked him or not, at first, because he was quiet until you got to know him. He had a conservative black Ford coupe, with Michigan license plates, and he dressed like a businessman rather than a college boy.

Frank and Bill had moved out of their room again, and doubled up with Fred and Dan. When Doctor Bob found out about that, he made Frank move back with him.

"For the last ten years I've been living in fraternity houses and hospitals," he said. "I wouldn't feel at home in a room all by myself. And there's no need for you four to be crowded up like that."

The bathtub maneuver, with Frank masquerading as a girl, had worked so well on Al that the boys had considered trying it on Doctor Bob. But after he relieved the congestion in Fred's and Dan's room, they decided to drop the whole idea.

"It wouldn't work on him anyway," Bill explained. "If anyone walked in on him, he wouldn't mind. He'd probably say, 'Hi, Sis,' and go right on washing."

Tom stood in some awe of Anne's fiancé, since he was a doctor, although a young one. But the awe was not sufficient to prevent Tom from giving him a piece of his mind one night, when he found Doctor Bob sitting on his kitchen table.

Tom was particular about the table. It was his office, and it symbolized something that was exclusively his. He ate off it, kept his tools on it, and maintained a bed for Fourteen under it. Although Tom often cleaned chickens and skinned squirrels on his table, none of us was allowed to place anything unsanitary upon it, particularly ourselves.

Anne was preparing a midnight meal after the movies, and Doctor Bob was watching from the table, when Tom came down from his room to get a pitcher of ice water.

"My table," Tom gasped. "Get your hiney offen there."

"Don't pay any attention to him, Bob," Anne blushed. "He does that to everybody."

"I have to eat my food offen there, you know," Tom screamed.

"You're not dealing with children any more," Anne told him furiously. "You go back to your room and be quiet."

"I quit," Tom shouted, reaching behind him in a familiar gesture to untie his apron, but finding only the rear of his bathrobe. "Let your Mother find someone else to do all the dirty work around here."

"Wait a minute," said Doctor Bob, sliding off the table, "I'll sit in a chair. There's nothing to get excited about."

Tom seized a dishrag and a bar of soap, and scrubbed the table officiously.

"I wouldn't mind if I didn't eat offen here," he kept mumbling. "It's bad enough having members of the immejate family sitting on it."

"I don't blame you," sympathized Doctor Bob, who had heard from Anne about Tom's ideas concerning his own illnesses. "A man who's been through what you've been through can't be too careful about germs."

"That's right," Tom agreed, somewhat mollified. "But nobody around here don't consider that. How did you know?"

"Come over here in the light." Doctor Bob spread open one of Tom's eyes and peered into it. "Now open your mouth and say 'ah.' "

Tom opened his mouth and said it.

"Clear history of pleurisy. You're in good shape now, but watch the germs. If you ever feel an attack coming on, there's an old medicine on the market that's better than any of the new things. It's called . . ."

"Quinine Remedy," Tom beamed.

Doctor Bob nodded sagely.

"Yes, *sir*," said Tom, sucking in his stomach, and spreading newspapers over his table. "You can sit up here, now, Doctor, if it's more comfortable."

"I'm all right, here in the chair."

"Come on, sir," Tom begged. "Make yourself comfortable."

Doctor Bob climbed back on the table.

"For Pete's sake," Anne said incredulously. "You're the first one he's let do that since Dad died."

"I don't mind when there's papers on the table," Tom explained patiently. "I used to spread out papers for your father, too. I got to eat offen there, you know."

"You can't be too careful," Doctor Bob agreed.

By the second day of Doctor Bob's visit, all of us had decided we wanted him as a member of the family. So much so that we began to take precautions to make certain Anne wouldn't lose him.

Frank, Bill, and Fred drew up a schedule and stood watch in the mornings, so that no one would make any noise and awaken Doctor Bob. Frank had the duty on the second floor, Bill on the first, and Fred outside his window. Tom fixed special desserts for him, and was always sending milk and sandwiches up to his room.

Some mornings, when he was up before Anne, Doctor Bob would play baseball with the boys or take the girls riding in his car.

"Are you sure you're having a good time?" we'd ask him. "Would you like us to call Anne, now? She's slept long enough. Ordinarily, she's up with the birds, doing all the housework."

"No, that's all right. Let her sleep."

"And, boy, is she a good cook!"

"I'll bet," he'd grin.

"Is there anything we can get you? How about another cup of coffee?"

"No thanks. I'm doing fine."

Anne finally complained about it to Mother.

"He's going to think they're all dying to get rid of me," she moaned.

"He's got more sense than that," Mother said.

"It used to be, when I had a fellow over, that I couldn't get rid of the kids. They'd be all over me, or hiding under the sofa, or peeking through the keyhole, or making loud sounds of kisses every time anyone tried to hold my hand."

"I know it," Mother sympathized. "And your father used to egg them on. I used to speak to him about it."

"I know you did. I'm not blaming you. But I'll swear all that was better than what they do now. When we walk into a room now, they all nudge each other, when they think we're not looking, and then get up and leave. It's almost indecent."

Mother shook her head and tried not to smile. "They're the limit," she agreed.

"They invent all kinds of excuses about why they have to leave. The lamest you ever heard—and they expect him to swallow them. Like, it's high time they taped the handle of their baseball bat. Or they'd better go check and see whether Fourteen has had kittens. Or they promised Tom they'd help him sift the ashes."

Then There Were Ten

"It's hard to be the oldest," Mother agreed.

"If Bob and Jane don't get the hint, the others pick them up bodily and carry them out. And then Frank and Bill mumble something about saving electricity, and go around switching out the lights. My shins are all barked up from bumping into things in the dark."

"It just means the children like Doctor Bob," Mother said. "It's a compliment to him, really, dear."

"But suppose," Anne groaned, "he gets the idea that all that business of turning off the lights has been going on with every boy I've ever had over here before?"

Doctor Bob liked children and knew how to talk with them. Bob and Jane started following him around the house, and wouldn't go to bed at night unless he'd come up and tuck them in. Although we tried to keep them out of the way, they started begging to be taken along when he and Anne went out in his car in the afternoons. Bob would sit between Doctor Bob and Anne in the coupe, and Jane would sit on Anne's lap. We were horrified, but the two youngest children wouldn't listen to reason.

"I give up," Anne told her fiancé, on one such afternoon excursion. She adjusted Jane on her lap. "Either they're in our hair, like right now, or they're tiptoeing around turning out lights."

"I don't mind it either way," her Bob chuckled. "Except I never saw a house where they had more baseball bats to tape or more ashes . . . Look, Bobby," he said, pointing out his window. "See the choo-choo train?"

"Where?" said Bob, leaning across him. "Where, Doctor Bob?"

"We just passed it. Look out the back window, and you'll see it."

Bob stood up on the seat and then, so he could get a better view, stood on Doctor Bob's thigh. "Choo, choo, choo," he said. "Big son of a gun, isn't it, Doctor Bob?"

"It sure is. One of the biggest."

"At one time," said Anne, "I was silly enough to think that by the time I was engaged I might occasionally ride in an automobile without holding children in my lap. I used to have dreams, when I was a little girl, of sitting up front and having a whole half-seat, all to myself. I used to dream . . . Look, Janey, see the horsey?"

"Where, Anne? I don't see the horsey?"

"We just passed it," said Anne, holding her up so she could look out the back window.

Doctor Bob reached over and squeezed Anne's hand. Her diamond solitaire picked up a piece of the sun and sparkled.

They were married in September of the following year, after Anne had received her diploma. The wedding was at our house. At Anne's insistence, Mother herself gave the bride away.

The minister of our church in Montclair, who was to officiate at most of our weddings and a dozen or so christenings of Mother's grandchildren, performed the ceremony.

The minister had children of his own, and a good deal of poise. He wasn't upset when Lillian and Fred blundered into the room that had been assigned to him, while he was slipping into his vestments. And he chuckled, along with everyone else, when young Bob jumped onto Anne's train and brought the wedding procession to a faltering halt.

It was a happy wedding, but we felt sorry for Mother. We thought we knew what was running through her mind. Anne was the first to leave the fold. Ernestine and Martha would probably be next. How would Mother get along with a family

of only eight children? How would she feel when all of the children, even Jane, had married and left home?

Poor Mother, we thought. Poor, poor Mother.

Tom watched the ceremony from the back of the crowd, occasionally producing a none-too-clean handkerchief to dab at his eyes. When it was over, he pushed his way up to Anne, fished in his pocket, and handed her twenty crumpled one-dollar bills.

"If he ain't good to you," he said, "I want you to buy a ticket and come home."

Anne looked for a minute as if she might lean over and kiss him, but Tom went into his fighter's crouch, weaving and making fierce faces.

"If he don't behave hisself," said Tom, "let him have the left like I learned you, and follow it with the right, like this."

He feinted twice at Doctor Bob, who made believe he was baffled and completely helpless under the onslaught.

"If I find him with so much as an elbow on my kitchen table," Anne promised, "I'm sending for you."

It wasn't until Anne and Doctor Bob got their suitcases and started for their coupe that Jane and Bob realized the newly-weds were going away on a trip.

"Take us with you, Doctor Bob," they begged, lunging for his legs. "You haven't taken us for a ride all day."

He lifted up Jane and kissed her, and looked helplessly at Anne.

"No, sir," said Anne, trying to disentangle them. "Not on our honeymoon. On that I positively draw the line."

17

POP AND THE WEASEL

MARTHA had contacts, although she never went out of her way to develop them. She knew the mayor, the mayor's secretary, librarians, store managers, motormen, policemen, delivery boys, and firemen.

With Anne married and Ernestine at Smith, Martha took charge of the household when Mother was away on business, and stretched the budget farther than it ever had gone before. Without spending any more money, she saw to it that each of us got a few more of the things he wanted.

Martha ran the house in the same manner that she performed her school work—effortlessly and efficiently, but without pretense of perfection. She saw to it that the necessary and important things got done. And she refused to allow the unnecessary or unimportant ones to cause her any concern.

If she could settle for a "B" or a "C" in a school subject, she saw no point in slaving for an "A." Of course, if an "A" came naturally, and occasionally one did, so much the better.

Likewise, if we swept and dusted the house in the mornings,

[175]

she saw no reason to nag if we sometimes forgot to wipe our feet or hang up our overcoats when we got home from school in the afternoons. Besides, sometimes she wasn't too careful about wiping her own feet, or hanging up her own overcoat.

Martha's contacts in Montclair made things easier for all of us. She'd get the grocer's delivery boy to stop by the hardware store to pick up something we had bought. She'd ask the men who drove the city's snow plows if they'd mind taking a few minutes to clear our driveway. If Tom were sick, she'd get the milkman to help Frank and Bill carry the furnace ashes from the basement to the yard.

People seemed to like doing things for her, and Martha didn't mind helping them. She knew whom to call if a street light were broken, or if the garbage man had forgotten to come by our block, or if a rabid dog were reported in the neighborhood. Mother, and even the neighbors, began to depend on her when they wanted something done by the town.

Once when Mother was out of town, a sleet storm broke the power lines and the utility company said service couldn't be restored for twenty-four hours. Martha called the fire chief and asked him what to do.

"With all the children we have in the house," she told him, "I thought it might be a fire hazard to have them stumbling around in the dark striking matches."

A fire truck pulled into the driveway a few minutes later with six electric lanterns, on loan to Martha. She had a thermos of coffee ready to send back to the station to the chief.

Martha studied the budget periodically to discover just where the money went, and to see if she could fix it so that less of it went there. If she couldn't figure out a way herself, she'd call the person who was getting the money, and ask him.

For instance, there was the matter of hair cuts. As Martha

pointed out, it was a relatively small item, but one that re-curred. She telephoned the owner of the barber shop frequented by the boys, and explained her problem.

She told him that, since we had six boys, we had to spend more money on haircuts than most families—that it usually came to at least $3 a month. She wondered whether there was any way he could give us a special rate. And if it wouldn't pay him to make us a rate, did he know anybody who was just opening a shop, and needed the business, who might be willing to do so.

The barber said he never had given special rates before, but that he wouldn't mind doing it provided the boys didn't come on weekends or after five o'clock in the afternoons, when business was heaviest.

Money saved on transactions such as that was available for luxuries. If any of us wanted anything badly enough, and it didn't cost too much, Martha would try to get it, and still keep within the budget. If she turned us down, we could always go to Mother, who usually would see that we got what we wanted whether the budget could afford it or not. But Martha, ordinarily easy going, became furious when any of us worried Mother about money matters. And we found it was advisable, if we were going to expect favors from Martha in the future, not to go over her head.

Whenever possible, and if the price were right, we did business with the United Cigar Store, which gave out coupons and certificates with each sale. The Cigar Store had a catalogue of premiums that included almost everything any of us wanted.

There were such items as a Genuine Cowhide, Jet Black, Positively Guaranteed, Big League Catcher's Mitt, for 415 certificates. And the catalogue said that in addition to the mitt, a regulation big league baseball would be given away absolutely free, for a limited time only, to boys taking advantage of this amazing offer.

Five yellow coupons equaled one green certificate, and we kept them in separate cigar boxes on Martha's dresser. Every couple of weeks, she'd call us into her room and we'd count what we had, putting rubber bands around each hundred coupons and each 20 certificates, and then figuring how long we'd have to wait until we had enough of them to redeem.

Tom was a chain smoker, and usually bought his cigarettes by the pack, at whatever store happened to be handy. He was continually running out of them, and borrowing from the men taking Mother's course, or smoking butts from the ashtrays.

Martha started buying cartons of his brand, at the United Cigar Store, and leaving them in the pantry. Whenever Tom took a pack, he'd put an IOU in the carton, and settle up with Martha on pay day.

"I never thought you'd try to make money off of me, like in a company store," he'd grumble as he paid his bills.

But Martha pointed out that she was selling him the cigarettes at cost—and that he was saving money by getting the carton rate. All she wanted was the certificates.

Tom really was pleased by the convenience of Martha's "canteen," but he went out of his way to check and re-check her addition, and to question the authenticity of his IOUs.

"That don't look like my writing," he'd say. "Where's that magnifying glass at?" Then, after he had paid with seeming reluctance and twice counted his change, he'd add: "Give me them IOUs so I can tear them up. I think some of these were the same ones you charged me for last week."

Mother's students found out about the supply of smokes, and began patronizing the pantry. Later, Martha started stocking razor blades, which were another item Tom usually forgot to buy.

The first premium we obtained with the certificates was a Mother's Day present, an ornate bedside lamp with a bright and dim switch. Mother used to say that Mother's Day was a ridiculous occasion, and that anyone who felt he had to give his female parent a special present, one day a year, must be trying to atone for 364 days of previous neglect.

We thought, though, she was telling us that so we wouldn't feel bad because we couldn't afford presents.

It took 650 certificates for the lamp. Mother seemed startled when we presented it to her. But when she found that we hadn't spent our allowances for it, or dipped into the budget, she was as pleased as if she had invented Mother's Day herself.

"When I think of you children saving those certificates for months, just so you'd have something to give me . . ." she began.

"You don't believe we're atoning for other days of neglect, do you Mother," Lillian asked her anxiously.

"No, I don't think that, dear," said Mother, and her voice broke. "I know how long you've been saving those certificates, and counting them at night, and . . . Well, I don't think there was anything to atone for."

After that we got the catcher's mitt, an electric toaster, ice skates and skis, a cigarette lighter for Tom, and finally a bottle-capper.

Martha decided on the bottle-capper so that the younger children could make their own soft drinks. The budget, in the past, hadn't been able to include root beer or ginger ale. But Martha knew the children were fond of soda pop, and would like to have it in the ice box to serve their friends. It still was out of the question for us to buy soft drinks at a store, because a case would have disappeared in a single afternoon. But if the children could make the drinks at home, the cost would be negligible.

Old gin, rye, White Rock, syrup, and bluing bottles were rounded up from the neighbors' basements, washed thoroughly, and then boiled in a tub on the kitchen stove. Some of the labels wouldn't come off, but we figured the bottles were clean on the insides.

Sugar was added to root beer extract, which in turn was poured into a vat of simmering water. Then a little yeast was added, and the mixture poured into the bottles. After the caps were applied, the bottles were stored in the basement for a week, and then were ready to drink.

The children thought, and so did their friends, that the root beer was the peer of any that came from the store. A new batch was made every couple of weeks, and finally a sort of assembly line technique was developed, with two children washing bottles in the basement, two boiling bottles on the stove, and two mixing the brew.

The empty bottles then were lined up around the stove, and the mixture siphoned into them through a rubber tube. We could make a couple of hundred bottles of root beer in less than forty minutes, and from that time on the basement always contained a batch that was ready to drink, and another batch that was aging.

Fortunately, Tom liked root beer, so there was no objection from him about dirtying up his kitchen. But as the weeks passed, he said he was getting mighty tired of the same old flavor.

The next time we made root beer, he suggested that we leave about a gallon of the mixture on the stove, so that he could change the flavor to suit his taste.

Pop and the Weasel

Tom added a package of prunes, a cup of sugar, and a whole yeast cake into the brew. Then he boiled it for half an hour, before siphoning it into the remaining bottles.

"I'm putting my name in chalk on these here bottles," he told us. "Don't nobody touch them, because I don't know how it's going to turn out. I'm going to leave them stand for six months, and see how the flavor is."

"You're sure you're not trying to make yourself some kind of home brew?" Frank wanted to know.

"Who, *me?*" Tom asked piously. "There's a law against that, ain't there?"

There was a law against it, all right. But after a day off in West Orange, Tom in the past had sometimes returned to the house smelling strongly of something that wasn't root beer.

Cousin Leora wasn't really a cousin, which was something to be thankful for. Her family and Mother's had been close friends and neighbors in Oakland, and she had married and moved East about the same time that Mother had.

She was plump, soft, bejeweled and inquisitive. None of us liked her, and Dad had despised her. He said she was a bloated drone, and that if the Bolshevists ever took over—which wouldn't surprise him—she'd be at the top of their purge list.

Cousin Leora's husband wisely had given up the ghost within a year of their wedding day. It was an action we felt sure he never regretted, although his worldly goods had been considerable. Left a widow with a sizable fortune, which flowed through her fingers like flypaper, she lived by herself in an apartment in New York.

Her visits to our house had become fairly frequent since Dad's death. Since she liked to quiz us about family affairs, she usually came when Mother was out of town. Invariably she arrived while we were eating supper. And, almost invariably, it would happen to be the one night of the week when we were relying on leftovers.

Once she had written Grosie, Mother's mother in Oakland, that she doubted if we were getting enough to eat. As a result, Mother had had a series of anxious telephone calls from Grosie asking if everything was all right, and if we needed money.

The calls had upset Mother so much that all of us tried to act particularly well-disciplined and well-fed, when Cousin Leora came to call.

A few months after we started to make our own root beer, Cousin Leora dropped in one night just as we had sat down to the table. Tom saw her chauffeur wheel the limousine into our driveway, and rushed into the dining room to spread the alarm.

"Everybody quiet down and behave hisself," Tom shouted. "It's the fat old snoop from New York."

"Not," gasped Martha, clutching her head, "Cousin Leora! How could she know this is hash night?"

"I think she likes my secret reseat," Tom said proudly. "I believe Old Snoop can smell my hash all the way acrost the Hudson."

"Open some cans of vegetables," Martha hollered as she dashed into the front hall to hang up overcoats and to kick arctics and ice skates into a closet. "And everybody pick up his dishes and put on a Sunday tablecloth."

Cousin Leora entered the hall without ringing the bell.

"Why look who's here," Martha cooed. "Cousin Leora! What a lovely surprise. I do hope you'll stay for supper."

Cousin Leora would stay, she said, providing she wouldn't be depriving the dear children of their food. Martha took her things, and by the time they entered the dining room the table was reset on a starched linen cloth.

Mother had spoken that afternoon in Philadelphia, and still hadn't gotten home. But we were expecting her shortly, and Tom was keeping her dinner warm. Cousin Leora didn't seem displeased by Mother's absence. In fact, we thought we detected a gleam of satisfaction in her eyes.

"Your dear Mother's hardly ever home any more, is she?" Cousin Leora began as Frank helped her into her chair.

"She's here almost every day," Martha said. "She has her Motion Study Course right here in the house, you know. I think this is the first time she's been away in a month or more."

"I see," our guest nodded, setting in motion a series of chins which broke like waves on the expansive beachhead of her bosom. But she pursed her lips and made it plain she didn't believe a word of it.

"I'm afraid," Martha stumbled, "we're having hash again tonight. You always seem to have the bad luck of picking a hash night."

"Hash seems good to me, after all that rich food we've been having," said Frank, trying to help out.

"There, there, dears," Cousin Leora comforted us. "You don't have to make excuses to me. I'm practically one of the family. I know things have been difficult since your father passed away."

"Not that difficult," Martha smiled weakly, trying to remember that she mustn't act undisciplined. "We had roast pork last night, and meat loaf the night before that."

"I'm sure you did, dear." Cousin Leora pursed her lips again.

"If she's sure we did," Fred whispered to Dan, "why does she make an ugly face like that?"

Cousin Leora had good ears, and she didn't miss much.

"Gentlemen don't whisper at the table," she reproved Fred. "I said I was sure you did, and I was not aware that I made an ugly face."

"I'm sorry," Fred apologized. "But we did. Ask anybody."

Martha wanted to side with Fred, but even more she wanted to prevent Mother's being upset by any new telephone calls from California.

"Whispering isn't polite, and Cousin Leora certainly wasn't making faces," she told Fred. "If you can't behave yourself, you'll have to leave the table and go without your supper."

"Goodness, don't take the food away from the poor child," Cousin Leora protested, in a tone indicating our rations were so scanty that missing a meal might bring on pellagra. "Perhaps it would be better if we change the subject. What do you hear from your grandmother, dear?"

"She's just fine," said Martha, welcoming the change and clinging to it tenaciously. "Yes, sir, just fine. Grosie is fit as a fiddle. She sure is."

"I've known your grandmother ever since I was a little girl. She's a lovely person, isn't she?"

"We certainly think so," Martha agreed. "We certainly do. They don't make them any sweeter than Grosie."

"And quite well off financially, isn't she? I suppose she's very generous."

"She sends us lovely presents," Martha nodded.

"But I know she must be generous in other ways, too. Generous in making things easier for your Mother."

"She's certainly offered to make things easier," Martha nodded again.

"I thought she must have," Cousin Leora smirked. "With two girls in college and this big household to run. . . . I suppose your Mother has had to rely on her rather heavily, hasn't she?"

"I guess you mean," Martha said as civilly as she could, "does Mother rely on her for money."

"Of course, it's none of my business," Cousin Leora tittered nervously, "but your Mother is such a dear friend of mine."

Fred leaned over when he thought no one was looking, and whispered something else to Dan, this time so quietly that no one heard.

"I saw that," Cousin Leora snapped. "What was that you said, young man?"

"Nothing, I guess," Fred mumbled.

"I want to know what you said. Speak up!"

"Do I have to tell her?" Fred asked Mart. "It's going to make her mad."

"I guess you'd better tell her," Martha nodded sympathetically.

"I said," Fred stuttered, looking at his plate, "if you're such a good friend of Mother's, why don't you ask her?"

Dan decided to give Fred what moral support he could. He made up his mind that since Cousin Leora was already convinced we didn't get enough to eat, he might as well give her something interesting to put in her letters to California.

"If Fred has to leave the table for whispering," Dan asked, "can I have his hash? I've lost more weight than anyone else this year."

Fred bared his teeth and growled in mock ferocity. "If you touch it, I'll bite you," he snarled.

"Goodness," said Cousin Leora.

"That's enough, boys," Martha warned sternly. "And if anybody gets the hash, I'm going to be the one. I'm the oldest, so I need the nourishment more than anyone else."

We heard Mother coming up the front steps, then, and ran out to meet her. Bill took her coat and hat, and Tom brought in her plate from the kitchen. Mother said the speech in Philadelphia had gone fine, and that she was so glad, this time, not to miss Leora.

"I love hash," Mother announced enthusiastically, and partly for Tom's benefit, as she sat down at the table. "And I love to get home after a train ride. Well, what were you talking about when I came in?"

"Nothing much," Martha put in hastily. "Just chatter."

"As a matter of fact, Lillie," Cousin Leora told Mother darkly, "we were discussing whether this one"—she pointed a diamond-studded finger at Fred—"should leave the table."

"Why, Freddy!" Mother said softly. "What did you do, dear?"

"I whispered," Fred admitted. "I didn't think anybody was looking."

"It's not polite to whisper," Mother announced, relieved that the offense hadn't been something more serious. "You know when I was a girl, and we whispered at the table, my father used to make us say it out loud. Sometimes," she laughed, "it was mighty embarrassing, too."

"That's what Cousin Leora made me do," said Fred.

It all sounded rather gay to Mother—not serious at all. "And what were you whispering about?" she asked, laughing again.

"Harumph," Cousin Leora cleared her throat noisily.

"Well," said Fred, "she wanted to know if you got money."

"What group were you speaking to in Philadelphia, Lillie, dear?" Cousin Leora interrupted.

But Mother was listening to Fred. "Who wanted to know if I got money, Freddy?"

"Harumph, harumph," said Cousin Leora.

"Cousin Leora wanted to know if Grosie sent you any money, and I whispered that if she wanted to know that, she ought to ask you."

Nobody said anything for a minute. Our guest looked as if she had swallowed some of her hash the wrong way, and Mother stared at her with something that was part wonder and part contempt.

"I'm going to answer your question, Leora," Mother said finally. "I haven't been getting money from California. They've offered, of course. But so far I've been able to handle things by myself. And I think the worst of it is over."

Cousin Leora glared defiantly. We knew she never had liked us, and now we knew she didn't like Mother, either.

"You haven't been able to handle it," she spit out spitefully, "when your children don't even get enough to eat."

If she had sat down and rehearsed that speech from the day she had learned to talk, she couldn't have come up with anything that would have made Mother any angrier. But Mother decided she wasn't going to lose her temper in front of her children. She felt around with her foot for the bell under the carpet, pressed it, and asked Tom to bring in the dessert. The left side of her mouth was twitching, or trembling—we couldn't be sure which. It was the first time we had ever seen it act that way.

Tom came in, heavy laden with a tray of chocolate blancmange. Perhaps it was the vibration of his footsteps; perhaps it was chance. At any rate, there was a booming, house-shaking roar in the basement, followed by a metalic ping as something hit the basement ceiling, directly below us.

Cousin Leora jumped out of her chair in terror, and even Mother dropped her fork.

"Earthquake," croaked Leora, who had been through the San Francisco one. And then much louder, "Earthquake!"

There were four more window-rattling roars, each followed

[187]

by a ping, and then we heard something flowing and dripping, down below us.

"Listen at that," said Tom. "It ain't no earthquake. It ain't nothing to get excitet about."

"What in the world is it then?" Mother demanded sharply.

"It ain't nothing but the children's beer," he assured her.

"Mercy Maude," sighed Mother. "It gave me a start."

"The children's what?" shrieked Cousin Leora. "Did he say the children's beer?"

"Root beer," Mother explained, and the left side of her mouth was vibrating again. "They make it themselves."

"Root beer," said the visitor, edging toward the hall, "doesn't explode. Only something with alcohol in it explodes. I don't think it's safe in here."

She opened the door to the hall, and an unmistakable aroma of alcohol permeated the dining room.

"So you've even let your children do that, have you?" she called over her shoulder as she went to get her wraps. She grabbed them and started for the front door. "I'm going to write your mother about you, Lillie Gilbreth."

The door slammed and two more bottles exploded. We heard gravel spatter as the limousine rolled out of the driveway.

Mother was simply furious. Psychologist and doctor of philosophy she might be. But now, just for once, both her psychology and her philosophy deserted her.

"Let her go ahead and write her, then," Mother mumbled. "See if I care. My folks have more sense than to believe anything like that. Let her go ahead and write a whole book. See if I care."

"Don't let her upset you, Ma'am," said Tom. "She ain't nothing but a fat old snoop."

"Fat old snoop," Mother repeated, as if that was what she

had been looking for. "Fat old . . ." She glared at Tom, who started nervously dealing out the blanc-mange.

"Let's hear from you," she said, and we had never heard her talk like that before. "Where did that alcohol smell come from?"

"All right, Ma'am," Tom conceded, and he was gaping like the rest of us. "It must have been one of them bottles I put prunes in. Just to change the flavor, of course."

She asked Tom to step into the kitchen with her. She closed the door behind her, but we could hear the rise and fall of her voice. And then we heard Tom sob, and go up the back steps toward the attic, where his room was.

When Mother returned, she was pale and shaking. She wasn't furious any more.

"I had to do it," she told us. "I had to let him go. I know how you feel about him, but that's simply the last straw. I have enough on my mind, when I leave you children alone, without worrying about something like that."

No one felt much like eating dessert, or talking. We knew it was Mother's decision to make, and we didn't blame her. But we thought there'd be an empty place in the house without Tom.

He didn't have many things to pack, and pretty soon we heard him come down stairs again, and then descend into the basement.

Mother looked around the table miserably, but we avoided her glance.

"I told him to get rid of the bottles with the prunes in them, before he left," she explained.

We still didn't say anything.

"After he gets rid of the bottles," Mother sighed, "you go down there, Frank, and ask him if he wants his job back. Tell him that, just this once, I changed my mind."

18

MARCH ON WASHINGTON

WITHIN the next few years,
Mother became accepted as an industrial engineer, and motion
study began to play an increasingly important part in the mass
production of the Twenties.

The fight had been uphill, but many of Dad's former clients
—and a good many new clients—finally had conceded that
Mother knew her business, and had hired her firm as a con-
sultant. The family finances, while not in a state of great
prosperity, were immeasurably improved. Mother still rode
in buses and upper berths. But she was able to start paying off
her debts and to make a dent in the mortgage on the house.

Mother's goal of sending all of us through college now seemed
more than just a possibility. Martha was enrolled at New
Jersey State College for Women, and Frank at the University
of Michigan. That meant there were only Bill, Lillian, Fred,
Dan, Jack, Bob, and Jane to usher into the halls of higher
learning. Mother was sure it was going to be a breeze.

While Mother's nose was healing, she had started writing

March on Washington

The Home Maker and Her Job, published in 1927. *Living With Our Children* was published the following year. She continued to teach her Motion Study Course, served on the New Jersey State Board of Regents, and was a delegate to the World Power Congress in Tokyo.

She also became a Girl Scout.

Mrs. Herbert Hoover was responsible for Mother's original interest in scouting. Mother had known the Hoovers for a good many years; socially, since they were fellow Californians, and professionally, since Mr. Hoover was an engineer.

After Mr. Hoover was inaugurated president, Mother sometimes visited them in Washington and at their fishing camp on the Rapidan River. Mr. Hoover appointed her to his national advisory committee on employment. And Mrs. Hoover, who was national president of the Girl Scouts, wanted her to head up the personnel division of that organization.

Mother wasn't sure she could spare the time. But Mrs. Hoover invited her to a tea at which a delegation of ladies in uniform were present. In a surprise ceremony, Mrs. Hoover announced she wanted to take Mother into the Girl Scouts right then and there. With the other ladies smiling encouragement, Mother arose to recite the oath.

None of our girls had been scouts. But Frank and Bill both had joined the Boy Scouts some years before. Mother had helped them memorize their oaths and pass their tenderfoot tests.

Standing in the White House, she raised three fingers of her right hand. Mrs. Hoover nodded reassuringly. It was a solemn moment. Mother started to recite:

"On my honor, I will do my best to do my duty to God and my country always, to . . ."

The ladies snickered.

"That's fine," Mrs. Hoover smiled when Mother finished. "That means you're a full-fledged Boy Scout. Now would you like to join the Girl Scouts?"

Mother said she would.

"Girl Scouts *try*," said Mrs. Hoover. "Their oath starts like this. 'On my honor I will *try* to do my duty.'"

Mother raised three fingers again and swore to try. Later on, she even got a uniform. When our older girls teased her about it, and kept asking her to give her scout's honor every time she made a flat statement of fact, she'd threaten to buy khaki shirt and trousers and a campaign hat.

"I can always switch to the other branch, if you don't like this uniform," she'd say. "I took both oaths, you know."

On one of Mother's visits with the Hoovers, the President urged her to bring all of us to a formal afternoon reception at the White House. The affair was to be held within a few days, and was for the Cabinet, Supreme Court and the Diplomatic Corps.

"I'd like to meet all the Gilbreth children," the President said cordially.

Mother was grateful for the invitation. But she knew we didn't like appearing en masse at anything. Besides, she had visions of railroad tickets and new outfits for everybody.

"They'd all love to come," she said, "but I'm afraid they'd strain the seams even of the White House."

"Nonsense," said Mr. Hoover. "We'd love to have them."

"Suppose," said Mother, who thought a compromise was in order, "I just bring the six boys."

"The boys will be fine," Mr. Hoover agreed hopitably. "Why don't you telephone them right now? Come on. I won't take no for an answer."

A phone was thrust into Mother's hands, and she put in a

call for Montclair. Frank, who was home from the University of Michigan on a holiday, answered the ring.

"I have great news," Mother said, while the Hoovers beamed. "The President has been kind enough to invite all of you boys to a reception at the White House." She put her hand over the mouthpiece and turned to the Hoovers. "I can just see their faces, can't you?"

"For crying out loud," Frank groaned. "See if you can't get us out of it, Mother."

"I can't," said Mother. "I tried, but I can't. I can't believe it's true, either."

"I don't want to bring all those kids down there," Frank complained. "Besides, I've got a date for almost every night of my vacation."

"You'll have to break it, dear. You'll have to break the news gently so the other boys won't take the roof off the house when they hear the glad tidings. The Hoovers are right here, just think of that."

"Good night," said Frank, only much quieter. "I'm sorry. We're trapped then, eh?"

"You certainly are," said Mother. "We all are. It's not something that happens every day."

Mother told Frank she had business in Washington and wouldn't be able to return to Montclair to supervise the boys' preparations. They were to wear their best suits and of course white shirts and black shoes. If they took an early morning train from Newark, they'd get to Washington about lunch time. Mother would be waiting for them at her hotel, and they could come to her room and wash up, before the reception.

Bill, who was now a senior in high school and currently in charge of the checking account, withdrew enough cash from the bank to cover the cost of three full and three half tickets to Washington and return.

It seemed like a lot of money, and both Bill and Frank thought it would be cheaper to make the trip by car. They felt sure that, once they had arrived in Washington and had explained to Mother about the saving, she would approve too.

The two oldest boys and Martha were the possessors of a Model T touring car. The vehicle was an antique when they had acquired it the year before for $20, and it had aged perceptibly under its new ownership.

The car had neither top nor fenders. The body was painted airplane silver. A six-inch red stripe, none too expertly applied, ran waterline fashion around the hull at a point equidistant from the running boards and the top of the doors.

Starting the motor was a two-man proposition, with one person turning the crank and jiggling a wire-loop choke which protruded from the front of the radiator, and the other sitting in the driver's seat to retard the spark as soon as the engine coughed. But the three owners had done a good deal of work on the motor; it was reliable and purred like a kitten, only louder.

There was no doubt in anyone's mind that the car could make the trip to the Capital. As a matter of insurance, though, a pump, tire patches, spare spark coils, and miscellaneous tools were stowed under the seats. And the boys decided to start the journey before dawn.

The day before departure, Frank held a dress rehearsal to make sure that the delegation had the proper clothes. All of the boys, with the exception of Frank, owned blue serge suits. Frank had handed down his blue serge to Bill that autumn, and had replaced it with a collegiate number purchased at the Campus Toggery Shop, in Ann Arbor.

March on Washington

The suit had padded shoulders, wasp waist, 23-inch cuffs on the trousers, and a double-breasted vest with lapels. The color was something between tan and yellow, without many of the best features of either. The material was as heavy and hairy as an army blanket. It had cost $28, and Frank was immensely pleased with it.

From the consistency of the cloth, it was apparent that the suit would wear forever. It was this aspect that appealed least to the other boys, when Frank appeared at dress rehearsal.

"Good Lord, what's *that,*" Bill whinnied when Frank walked into the parlor. "I hope you didn't throw away the sales slip. Take it off quick, before you muss it up."

"What's the matter with it?" Frank asked with hurt feelings.

"If it's going to be a party like Hallowe'en," said Bob, who was nine, "can I wear my cowboy suit?"

Bill felt the material. "It's your own business what you buy when you get something thin that you can wear out yourself," he complained. "But when you pick out a heavy suit like that, you're supposed to have me with you."

"For something as heavy as that, he's supposed to take all of us with him," Fred added. "That one will go all the way down the line to Bob."

"What's the matter with you kids' taste?" Frank marveled. "How far behind the times is this town, anyway? This color is the latest thing at Michigan."

"It looks," said Bob, "like what happens to the mustard jar when you forget to screw the top back on."

"It does not," Frank told him, "and you keep out of this. It just happens I've had a lot of compliments on it at Michigan."

"You mean you've worn it before?" asked Bill, deflated. "Then you can't take it back?"

"I wore it all fall."

"How come I didn't see it in your closet after you unpacked?"

"Because I know you," Frank said. "That's why. Every time I get a new suit, the first thing I know you're borrowing it and spilling things on it."

"If he spilled mustard," Bob insisted, "you wouldn't have to worry, once it dried."

"It sheds, too," Bill said accusingly, picking nap off the sleeve of his blue serge, where it had brushed against Frank. "You're going to leave yellow hairs all over Mr. Hoover."

"I don't intend to be brushing up against anybody," Frank replied. "It sheds a little, I'll admit. That's because it's still comparatively new."

"Don't think I'm going to walk through the reception line with you," Bill warned. "I'm not going to watch cabinet officers and the diplomatic corps tiptoeing through great piles of nap that you've deposited all the way from the South Portico to the Blue Room."

"Do you think all the nap will be gone by the time it's handed down to me?" Bob asked.

"I doubt it," Bill replied. "I promise you one thing. I'll never help get rid of any of it."

There were two flat tires between Montclair and Philadelphia, but the boys patched them and the car ran well. Frank tried to make up some of the time they had lost in fixing the tires. Shortly before they reached Baltimore, a motorcycle patrolman came up behind them and waved them down for speeding.

"I congratulate you for bringing that heap all the way from New Jersey," he said, copying the license number into his ticket book. "If I didn't see it with my own eyes, I'd never believe you could get sixty miles an hour out of it."

March on Washington

"We can do seventy on the hills," Bob volunteered proudly. "Frank and Bill did something to make the engine run faster."

"Shut up," Bill whispered, leaning forward and beaning Bob with his knuckles. "Do you want to get us all sent up the river?"

"Sent up the river?" Jack sneered. "They can't do that to us. We don't take nothing from nobody, understand? Nothing from nobody?"

Bill beaned him, too.

"Seventy, eh?" said the policeman, making a note of it. He looked at the patched, treadless tires and shook his head. "What are you trying to do, Buddy, kill all those kids?"

At that point, Frank thought killing them was a pretty sensible suggestion. But he shook his head, gulped, and wondered how Mother would explain to the Hoovers that her sons couldn't attend the reception, on account of being sent up the river.

"Where do you think you're going, anyway?" the policeman asked thrusting his face up near Frank's.

"We're going to Washington, Officer."

"And what are you going to Washington for?"

Frank thought that one over, and concluded that if he knew what was good for him he'd better come up with a more convincing explanation than the truth.

"Why nothing in particular," he said. "Just to sight-see, I guess."

"Go ahead and tell him," Jack said contemptuously. "Don't let him buffalo you like that."

Bill beaned him again.

"Yeah, tell me," the policeman ordered.

"All right," said Frank. "We're going to see President Hoover."

"I love wise guys, particularly in suits like that one," the patrolman leered. "I suppose the President invited you, personal, to drop in and have tea with him at the White House? Sure he did."

Frank nodded sheepishly.

"Nothing from nobody," Jack repeated from the back seat, putting his hands over his head to try to stave off Bill's knuckles.

"That's right, honest," Frank said desperately. "We've had some flat tires, and we're late."

"You," said the policeman, pointing to Jack. "Is that right? Are you going to see the President?"

"Not just the President," Jack told him. "Mrs. Hoover and some judges from the Supreme Court, too. Why don't you shove off, Buddy?"

The patrolman surveyed the car, the airplane paint job, the red waterline. He looked at us individually—Frank, Bill, and Fred, greasy from changing tires. Dan pale and about to be car sick. Jack and Bob, wrinkled and dirty.

"I guess you're telling the truth," he said. "The President doesn't get many laughs, and I ain't going to be responsible for his missing this one. Go ahead. But not more than forty-five miles an hour."

The weather had been fair when the boys left Montclair, but it was cloudy in Baltimore, and between Baltimore and Washington it started to rain. The boys were wet through by the time Frank pulled up in front of Mother's hotel.

Even the Joad family never received a more wrathful reception from a doorman. He wouldn't let the boys alight until Frank promised to park the car down the street, a block away from the hotel.

Mother was sitting in an arm chair, reading and knitting, when the boys entered her room. She had already changed clothes, and was ready for the reception.

"Oh, my," she said.

"It's my fault, Mother," Frank told her. "I thought it would be cheaper and easier to drive."

"I don't mean that," Mother said. "Come here, Dan. You're pale as a sheet. You don't feel at all well, do you dear?"

Dan explained that he had been car sick, but that he felt all right now that he was on firm land again.

"You had me worried for a while," she smiled, kissing the boys. "You mean you drove all the way from Montclair in that gray thing. Won't Mr. Lindbergh be jealous!"

Frank said he was sorry that, because they were wet, they wouldn't be able to go to the reception. But Mother said they had to go, and that she thought she could dry them out on time.

"Everyone will look fine once they're dry," she added, "except . . . What's the matter with your suit, Frank? Did the rain fade it?"

"That's the way it looks all the time," Bill said resentfully.

"There's nothing the matter with it," Frank pouted. "It's the latest thing."

Mother said she was sure it was. She stripped her bed and gave each of the boys a sheet or blanket. They went into the bathroom, took off their clothes, and then sat around in bedware while they waited their turns to get baths.

Mother called the desk and made arrangements for an iron and ironing board to be sent up to her room, and for the boys' shoes to be taken down to the boiler room to dry.

"Oh, yes," she added as an apparent afterthought, "and send up a newspaper too, if you will."

After the board had been set up, Mother started pressing the boys' underwear, socks, shirts and suits until they were dry. She saved Frank's suit until the last. When she had finished with his coat and vest, and was in the middle of his pants, she stopped long enough to phone the desk again and ask that the shoes be returned.

A musty odor of burned dye and scorched wool permeated the room.

"Hey," shouted Frank. "My pants!"

Mother put down the phone quickly and ran to the board.

"Now look what I've done," she reproached herself. "I've burned a hole right through your beautiful trousers."

"Hot dog," Fred gloated.

"Ruined," Frank choked. "I'll never be able to match them."

"There's no argument there," Bill said.

"I don't know how I could be so stupid," Mother complained, looking at her watch. "We still have fifteen minutes, though. We'll pick up a new suit for you. I'll take along a needle and thread, and hem the cuffs so they'll do for the time being."

"Do you think we can find one with that heavy kind of material?" Frank asked.

"I hope we can. Say, it's lucky I had them send up a newspaper! Look through it and see if anyone's having a sale."

"Wait a minute," Frank said accusingly. "That business of ordering a newspaper. Are you sure that was just luck? You didn't burn those pants on purpose, did you?"

"For goodness' sake," Mother laughed. "Do you think I like to buy you boys new clothes? Do you think I'm naturally destructive?"

The shoes arrived from the boiler room. With Frank self-consciously holding down his coat, to hide a wedge-shaped hole in his trousers, Mother and the boys walked to a department store that had advertised a clothing sale. Frank found a suit of heavy material, not unlike his old one, except that it was conservatively cut and dark blue instead of yellow-tan.

Even Bill admitted it was handsome. The coat and vest fitted well enough, and Mother basted in the cuffs.

They stopped in a barber shop for shoe shines, and then hailed a cab.

"To the White House, please," Mother said. She looked as cool and unruffled as she had when the boys first arrived at her hotel.

The boys were on their especial good behavior as they waited to go through the receiving line. But when Bill saw an immensely dignified, bearded figure, he stage-whispered excitedly to Mother:

"Say, isn't that Charles Evans Hughes?"

The Chief Justice, who had heard his name, turned toward Bill and bowed formally from the waist.

"Good afternoon, Sir," he said, "and Madam."

If that was the way you behaved at the White House, the boys weren't going to be outdone. All six of them bowed from the waist, and said good afternoon, Sir.

The President and Mrs. Hoover were cordial and hospitable.

"They look just as if they'd stepped out of a bandbox," said Mrs. Hoover. "I never thought young boys could look that pressed." She turned to Frank. "You're the oldest, aren't you?"

Frank said he was, Madam.

"Then I guess you were the one who looked after everybody on the trip down. I guess you're the one I really ought to compliment about stepping out of a bandbox."

Frank said thank you, Madam. The boys bowed from the waist, and moved along the receiving line.

Mother had planned to return home by train that afternoon. Although she had always before avoided the Model T, she allowed herself to be talked into making the return trip in the car.

The skies had cleared and the weather was mild. Frank held the Ford at a dignified forty-five, and there was no tire trouble. They stopped at Baltimore for supper, and when they emerged from the restaurant the stars were out and it was still and peaceful.

"Why this isn't bad at all," Mother sighed contentedly. "I ought to let you boys drive me on all my trips."

They started to sing some of the songs Mother had taught them when they were younger. "Old Black Joe," "Clementine," "Backward, Turn Backward Oh Time in Thy Flight."

Half an hour out of Baltimore, a siren sounded and a motorcycle policeman pulled up along side.

"How was tea at the White House?" the officer hollered over the roar of two exhausts.

"Fine," Frank shouted back.

"How's the kid who was sick?"

"I'm fine," Dan assured him.

"And the one who don't take nothing from nobody?"

"Okay," Jack grinned.

The policeman gunned his motorcycle up the highway.

"Good gracious," Mother marveled. "I don't know how you boys do it."

They asked her what she meant.

"The Chief Justice of the Supreme Court bows to you, the President and his wife hold up a receiving line to chat with you, and you make friends with policemen all the way from Montclair to Washington. I'm certainly lucky to have such fine sons."

The boys had the good grace to think there was a slight possibility Mother might be prejudiced.

19

MOTHER WAS THERE FIRST

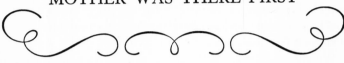

THOSE of us who were away at college usually saw Mother three or four times a semester, as her lectures and business engagements took her across the country.

Sometimes she'd be delivering a speech at the college itself, and would arrange her schedule so she'd have a free day to visit. Sometimes her speech would be at a city near one of the colleges, and it was possible to cut classes, hear her lecture, and then visit with her at her hotel.

Mother knew most of the presidents and many of the professors at the various colleges we attended. Usually, too, she knew the location of all the campus buildings, their nicknames, and the geography of the town.

It was somewhat disillusioning for a wide-eyed freshman, importantly taking his female parent on a sight-seeing tour of an institution which he was sure would overwhelm her with its unique traditions and maze of modern complexities, to discover that she knew more about his university than he did.

Mother Was There First

The home economics building? The "Home Ec" building certainly was one of the most modern in the country, Mother would agree. And it would develop that she had made a speech in the building last year, and had been on the program the year before when they dedicated it.

The stadium? "Old Horseshoe" was mighty impressive, she would nod. Under cross-questioning, she might point out that she had received an honorary degree in ceremonies in the stadium a few years before.

We chose our own colleges, but in most cases Mother had preceded us in the commencement parade.

She had degrees from a dozen or more institutions, including Michigan, where Anne, Frank and Jane were graduated; Smith, Ernestine and Lillian; Rutgers, the male half of Martha's college, New Jersey State College for Women; Purdue, Bill; and Brown, Fred.

To finish calling the roll, Dan received his diploma from the University of Pennsylvania, Jack from Princeton, and Bob from the University of North Carolina.

Mother never sent tuition checks directly to our colleges. At the start of each year she'd turn over to us, in one lump sum, enough money for our tuition and all other expenses. When you took out your own checkbook and paid the college registrar your tuition, you realized you were supposed to get something for your money. All of us did all right in college.

Mother spoke most often at Purdue, in West Lafayette, Indiana, where Bill was enrolled. Purdue was opening a motion study laboratory, and Mother was going to become a professor of management there. She intended to take the new job in addition to all her old ones, and to commute from Montclair to the campus once a month, for a week or so of teaching.

[205]

On one occasion when Mother was at Purdue, she was asked unexpectedly to speak before a large lecture class in which Bill was enrolled. Bill didn't know about the invitation. It was an eight o'clock class, and he picked that particular morning to oversleep.

Bill's professor told the students they were fortunate in having a distinguished engineer in their midst. She was Dr. Lillian Gilbreth, and it was gratifying to him that one of Dr. Gilbreth's sons was a member of that very class, and doubtless intended some day to follow in his mother's footsteps.

He cleared his throat and started to call the roll. All the way from the "A's" down to the "G's," Mother's eyes roved the auditorium, searching for Bill. She was sitting on a platform, in a chair next to the professor's table.

"Gibbes," said the professor.

"Here."

"Gilbert,"

"Here."

"Gilbreth."

There was an awkward pause, while Mother blushed and stopped searching. The professor looked up, cleared his throat again, this time with disapproval, and repeated loudly, "Gilbreth?"

A number of Bill's friends sensed the situation simultaneously, and thought they had better come to the rescue.

"Here," a dozen voices answered from all corners of the room.

The professor put down his roll book and looked bleakly at Mother. He didn't say so, but she gathered the look was intended to convey that he had to put up with a great deal, not the least of which was having Bill as a student.

Mother Was There First

He glared at his audience, seeking to find the offenders who had answered to Bill's name.

"There seem to be," he said sarcastically, "a good many Gilbreths here today."

"The whole family," Mother announced brightly, regaining her poise and favoring him with her warmest smile. "That's nice."

The professor, who hadn't seen as much of Bill that semester as he thought he should have, didn't think it was nice at all. He licked his pencil and made a show of marking a large zero in his grade book, opposite Bill's name.

"Goldsmith," he said precisely, continuing the roll.

Bill spent the afternoon and night with Mother, so he didn't see any members of the class during the remainder of the day. Mother didn't mention to him that she had spoken to his group, or that she knew he had cut the class. She thought he was old enough to make his own decisions, and that it wouldn't give him a sense of responsibility if she seemed to be checking up on him.

She did spend a good deal of time, though, telling him how she was studying the motions of physically disabled persons, so as to help them find jobs in industry. Bill was interested, and he and Mother looked over her notes and her photographs and diagrams of the project.

Bill was a little late, but present, for the lecture class the next morning. He slid into his seat just as the professor finished calling the "C's" in the roll book, and he was well settled by the time the professor reached the "G's" and finally Bill's name.

When the professor had run through the list, he told the class he was going to give a written quiz.

"I'm sure all of you must have learned a great deal from our visitor of yesterday," he said. "So today I'm going to ask you to write a little summary giving the high points of the talk."

Bill squirmed uncomfortably, and wished he had cut class again. He nudged the boy sitting next to him.

"Who," Bill asked out of the corner of his mouth, "did the old fool drag over here yesterday?"

"Are you kidding?"

"No, I wasn't here yesterday. I overslept."

"You overslept," the boy mimicked. "It was your own mother, you stupid jackass."

"Awk," Bill grunted, sinking down in his chair and wishing he could continue through the floor.

Everyone else in the room was writing. You could hear the pens scratching and papers rustling as pages were turned. Bill hoped no one would notice that he alone was sitting there doing nothing.

He nudged his neighbor again.

"Would you mind telling this stupid jackass," Bill apologized, "what my mother talked about?"

"Motion study of the disabled."

"Thanks," Bill grinned. He started writing, too.

20

PYGMALION

ALMOST every year there was a graduation from high school, a graduation from college, and a wedding. By the middle 1930's, all of us through Lillian were married and had homes of our own. Most of the married ones had children.

Fred and Dan were in college, Jack and Bob were in high school, and Jane was about to enter the tenth grade—the first year of high school under the system then standard in Montclair.

There was a New Deal in the country, and a New Deal at our house, where Jack was in charge when Mother was away.

The New Deal at home was brought about principally by Tom's absence. He was in a hospital, suffering from a heart ailment, and the warmth and excitement had evaporated from the kitchen. All rules about feeding and playing with Sixteen, his current cat, and about keeping out of the kitchen, except on Tom's special invitation, had been suspended.

An energetic colored woman now did the cooking, and as much of the housework and dishes as Mother would allow.

Mother always has been convinced that anyone who works for her is terribly imposed upon. So much so that sometimes it is difficult to tell who is working for whom.

As a result, it was a race between Mother and the energetic maid to see who could make the beds first and sweep the upstairs in the mornings. Since both were early risers, the race often ended in a dead heat, with Mother handling one side, and the maid the other, of a bed that was still warm.

"You have enough to do without making the beds," Mother would say when the maid urged her to sit down and relax for a few minutes. "This leaning over is just what I need. I like to get a little exercise before I leave for the city."

At supper time, Mother would whisk away a dish as soon as one of the children had taken his last mouthful, and carry it out to the butler's pantry to wash and dry it, while the maid was finishing her meal in the kitchen. When the child would go to put his fork down, there wouldn't be any place to put it except the table cloth, so he'd have to hold it in his hand until Mother came back.

"The maid may want to go to a movie or something," Mother would explain, while she collected the silverware. Between the colored woman and Mother, the children were relieved of all the chores that the rest of us had had to do in the past.

Now that there were no young children in the house, there was no need for the system under which each child was responsible for a younger one, or for the process charts in the bathrooms. The German and French language records had worn out or been broken, and Mother never replaced them.

When the married members of the family dropped in to visit, they didn't hesitate to tell Mother that they never had had things that easy when they were growing up, and that the three youngest ones were being spoiled.

Pygmalion

But Mother, bouncing a grandchild on her knee and playing peekaboo, would reply that she wasn't sure this little fellow was being raised just right, either. He had on too many clothes, for one thing, and she didn't think she liked his color. Those new formulas might be all right, but . . .

We knew it was an act, because Mother herself always laughed at meddling grandmothers, and she really believed that the new formulas were resulting in bigger, stronger babies. But she managed to get across her point.

We began to suspect, while watching how Mother was raising her three youngest, that she never had entirely approved of many of Dad's systems of regimentation. Some of them had been necessary because the family was so large. Perhaps she had allowed the others to remain in effect, until they stopped of their own accord, because she didn't want to overrule Dad.

Mother seemed, if possible, to grow closer than ever to her three youngest children. But we thought the house must seem empty of children to her. She was bound to realize that Jane would be away at college in a little more than three years, and that after that there would be no one left at home.

We wondered what she'd do in the big, drafty house that held so many memories. She couldn't stay there by herself, of course. Yet we felt sure she'd never be willing to sell it. And she had said repeatedly that she wouldn't live in anyone else's home—even the home of one of her children.

Frankly, we were worried about Mother.

The four youngest boys wanted to be sure Jane would be a social success when she entered high school. The last of the Gilbreths, they thought, should set a record for popularity that would stand at least until the grandchildren came along.

The bobby sox era was making its debut, after a decade of

formal afternoon dresses, spike-heels and kinky permanent waves. The hep-cat and the square were about to take their places at opposite ends of the terpsichorean scale, and it was possible to cut a rug without having either carpet or scissors.

The boys wanted to be sure that Jane was among the first on the bandwagon.

In many respects, Jane was Martha all over again. She was tall for her age, didn't realize she had developed a figure, and was content to wear Lillian's hand-me-down dresses and shoes. Also she had a habit of flopping untidily into chairs and spreading her knees as wide as a chestnut tree.

But she was beginning to be interested in boys, and she listened willingly to the suggestions of Fred, Dan, Jack and Bob.

Fred and Dan, who as college men spoke with some authority, were the first to start grooming Jane for high school. During the summer, they began telling her what sort of clothes she should buy for her fall wardrobe.

"Those things you wear are all out of date," Fred said. "Only sad apples wear them any more. You want to get saddle shoes, sweaters and skirts, and those socks that just come to your ankles."

"I'm not going to dress like a little girl," Jane complained. "I can dress up more than that when I go to high school, can't I, Mother?"

"The boys usually know what they're talking about," Mother said doubtfully.

"Lillian has a silk dress she said I can have, and I thought I'd get some others like that," Jane pouted.

"You listen to what we're telling you," Dan ordered. "Those silk dresses are out. The college girls are wearing what Fred says, and you want to be one of the first in high school to dress that way."

Pygmalion

"The first impression you make in high school decides whether you're popular," Jack agreed. "The boys from the upper classes come down by the front door and give the new girls the once-over."

Jane also was to let her blonde hair grow and fix it page-boy. She was to stop that business of flopping into chairs as if she were playing a game of statues, and she wasn't to use any make-up except lipstick.

Fred studied her face critically.

"Dark red lipstick," he said. "That's the color for you. Right, Dan?"

"Dark red," Dan agreed. "Not too much of it."

"But Mother said I could wear all the make-up I wanted to when I got to high school," said Jane. "I don't know about all this little girl stuff. Did Mother put you boys up to this?"

"I didn't have a thing to do with it," Mother protested. "I don't approve of make-up, but everyone I've seen in high school paints like an Indian. If that's the way you want to look, it's your face. See if I care!"

"What everyone else does in high school is old stuff," Fred explained. "That's what we're trying to tell you. Do you want to be a sad apple?"

Jane said she guessed that if she had to be any sort of an apple, she'd rather not be a sad one.

Dan then showed her how she should sit down. He walked mincingly but with assumed nonchalance to a chair, turned around with a swing of his hips, rose on his tiptoes, sat down daintily with his knees together, and flounced as he adjusted an imaginary skirt.

"It's that kind of jump you give at the end that gets them," he explained. "You see you act and dress casually, as if you didn't know men existed. But really you're on the ball all the time. And little things like that jump at the end emphasize all of a girl's best assets."

Jane tried it, but the boys were far from satisfied. She tried it again, with no more success.

"Don't jump like someone left a hatpin in the chair," Dan winced. "I'll swear, I believe you're hopeless. Don't you know how to do a feminine flounce?"

"I did just like you did," said Jane, beginning to lose patience. "You jumped like something was in the chair, too, didn't he Mother?"

Mother, sitting in a corner, pretended she was absorbed in a book, and didn't answer.

"I'm not supposed to know exactly how to do it," Dan shouted. "All I can do is give you the general idea. For Lord's sake, don't girls have any natural instinct about how to do things like that?"

"If they do," Jane said hotly, "it's the first time I ever heard about it. And I'm not going to listen if you holler at me. And I'm not going to dress that way, either."

She stalked across the room, picked up a magazine, sat down by Mother, and—there was no doubt about it—flounced as she angrily adjusted her skirts.

"That's it, Jane," Fred shouted. "Just like that."

"Just like what?" Jane sulked. "You give me a pain in the neck, all of you."

"What you did just then," said Fred, "when you fixed your skirts."

"I didn't do anything," said Jane, "except this." She flounced again.

"Solid," Dan agreed.

"Well, why didn't you say so. Anybody knows how to do that." She flounced a third time. "The way Dan showed me,

Pygmalion

you'd need a built-in pogo stick. I thought you were supposed
to see light between me and the chair."

Somewhat pleased with herself, she rejoined the boys for
further instruction.

Jane already knew most of the new dance steps, so her
brothers weren't worried about that. But they spent a good
deal of time teaching her dance floor behavior.

The boys thought that the most important formula for popularity at a dance was knowing how to act when someone cut
in. They said they had seen many a girl who was good looking
and a beautiful dancer, but who was stuck most of the night
because she had given the impression she didn't like to be
broken.

"It boils down to this, and I'll admit it's an art," said Dan.
"You've got to make the boy you're dancing with think you're
sorry that someone is cutting in; and you've got to make the
boy who's cutting in think you're glad."

Jane said that sounded insincere to her, and she believed a
girl always should be sincere, didn't Mother.

Mother thought that one was safe enough.

"Yes indeed, dear," she said, coming out from behind her
book. "It's a mistake to be hypocritical."

"Of course you should be sincere," Fred agreed. "But you
can be glad and sorry at the same time, can't you? Like when
you graduated from Junior High?"

"Sorry to leave those infants?" Jane laughed condescendingly.
"I was only glad then. But I guess I see what you mean."

"Sure you do," Fred soothed her. "You're a smart chick."

"Okay," Jane surrendered. "How do you do it, then?"

Fred and Dan, both six feet and none too graceful, started
to dance, and Jack and Bob, not far from six feet and even less
graceful, prepared to take turns cutting in.

Mother now gave up all pretense of reading. Her book lay face down on her lap. She had that what's-this-generation-coming-to look on her face, and she seemed tensed, as if ready to make a game try at catching the vases and lamps, in case the boys should bump into them.

"Now I'm leading," Fred told Jane, "and it's up to the girl to make small talk—about anything at all."

"The only small talk I'd make if you were my partner," said Dan, "is to warn you that if you didn't put your right hand up higher, I'd leave you in the middle of the dance floor. You wolf you!"

Jack stepped up and tapped Fred on the shoulder.

"Remember, Jane, I'm playing your part," Dan explained. "Up to now, you've been following your partner. Now you lead just enough so you swing him around, and your back's to the boy who cut in."

Dan swung Fred around.

"Only it's not absolutely necessary to kick him like that when you swing him," said Fred, rubbing his shins.

"Now," Dan continued. "See, my back's toward Jack. He can't see what I'm doing. So I look at Fred and I frown a little; I'm disappointed our dance had to end."

He wrinkled his forehead and nose, and made a hideous moue at Fred.

"See?" Dan asked Jane. "Now he thinks I hate to see him go. And he'll be pretty sure to come back and dance with me again."

"The hell I would," said Fred. "After that last look, I believe I'd run to the locker room and see if anyone had a drink."

"Then," Dan ignored him, "you separate from your partner. But notice you still hold his hand. Just before you let it go, you give it an intimate little squeeze, like this."

Pygmalion

Dan and Fred both squeezed, with all their might. They were always testing their grips, Indian wrestling, and putting their elbows side by side on a table to see which one could make the other bend his arm.

The handshake ended in a tie, and they let go.

"Now you turn around," said Dan, somewhat red of face but still intent on his instruction. "Your back's toward your old partner. Now you face your new partner, and your eyes light up. You've been rescued. You've been looking forward all night to this particular dance. You glide into your new partner's arms"—he stumbled into Jack's—"and you say . . ."

"Not yet you don't," Mother interrupted, and she was so intent her book toppled to the floor. "You've got to be careful to dance away a few steps from your old partner, first. You don't want him to hear you, do you?"

Dan let go of Jack, and all of them turned with new interest to Mother.

"How did you know that?" Fred asked. "You're completely right, but—why they didn't even cut in at dances when you were a girl."

"They didn't cut in," said Mother, "but they came up to your chair where you were sitting with your old partner. I always danced away a few steps from the chairs, and then I said . . ."

"Who's being hypocritical now?" Fred hooted.

"What was it you said, Mother?" Jane giggled.

"Nothing, I guess," Mother said primly, leaning over to retrieve her book. "Nothing that would interest this generation."

"Aw, come on, tell us," Jane insisted.

"Well," Mother blushed, "when it was your father, I guess I said something like, 'Why Mr. Gilbreth, imagine finding you here. Where have you been keeping yourself all evening?' "

"Was that before or after you were married?" Jane asked.

"Oh, both," said Mother, now apparently intent on her reading.

"And where had he been keeping himself?" said Jane, refusing to let the subject drop.

"What's that, dear?" Mother asked, as if she hadn't been paying attention.

"Where had he been?"

"Your father? Never very far away, dear," Mother smiled. "Not down in the locker room."

Jane's debut at high school was a success, and Jack and Bob informed her she had passed the opening day scrutiny. Besides Jane, only a handful of seniors had worn bobby sox clothes. But the handful was composed of girls who admittedly set the fashions, and there was no doubt that the new style would take hold.

Fred and Dan returned to Brown and Pennsylvania, respectively, and Jack and Bob continued the grooming of their youngest sister.

She was to be friendly with everybody, including sad apples and teachers. She was to learn the names of everyone in her classes, and to speak to them by name when she passed them in the halls. She was to be a good student, without giving the impression of studying too much. And she was to keep her face, hands and nails clean, even if it meant going to the girls' room between every class.

"There's nothing worse than a dingy-looking girl," Jack told her. "So don't think I'm minding your business if I see you in school and tell you to go wash yourself. I'll just whisper it."

"How about dingy boys?" Jane protested.

"Why Bob and I always look just like we stepped out of a bandbox," Jack smirked.

"I don't know about that," said Jane. "But if you did, you must have been playing the drums."

"Nobody notices how boys look," said Jack, cuffing her fondly. "And nobody cares whether boys are popular in school."

Sometimes Jane thought it was more trouble than it was worth, especially when the two boys said she might begin to put on weight, and so started taking her desserts away from her. But she had to admit they had been right about the clothes, and she suspected they knew what they were talking about on other things, too.

She started having movie dates at night, on week ends. Mother didn't disapprove, and Jack and Bob were elated. The boys wanted to make sure, though, that no one got the wrong idea about what sort of a girl she was, so they always told her just what time she was to be home. Usually, to make sure there was no misunderstanding, they told her date, too. When the date saw the size of her older brothers, and was informed that they'd be waiting up for Jane, there was little or no argument.

"Even Cinderella could stay out till midnight," Jane would complain to Mother. "Jack and Bob make my dates bring me home by 10:30."

"Your father wouldn't let Anne go out at all at night, unless he went along as a chaperone," Mother comforted her. "You don't know how lucky you are to have such liberal-minded men in the family."

"Good night, that was a generation ago. Times have changed!"

The first dance of the school year was a junior-senior-alumni affair, held during the Thanksgiving holidays. It was unusual for girls in the tenth grade to be invited—in fact none of our girls ever had been asked until they had become juniors.

But Jane's special popularity course had brought results. She had invitations from a junior and two seniors. The boys told her to accept the junior, since he had asked her first. The word always got around, they said, if you turned down an early invitation to accept a later one.

Fred and Dan were home for the holidays, and they and the younger boys agreed to go stag to the party, to make sure Jane wasn't stuck on the dance floor. Each of the boys also enlisted the aid of four or five friends, all of whom seemed willing, even eager, to cooperate.

Right from the start, Jane was broken more than any other girl. Her hand squeezes as she left one partner, and her pleased smiles as she started off with another, apparently became important factors as the night wore on. Because even without her claque, she was undeniably getting a rush.

Then Dan cut in, and found Jane near tears.

"He kissed me," she whispered indignantly. "I slapped him as hard as I could, and he just laughed and kissed me again."

Dan roughly shoved away two boys who were trying to cut in.

"Beat it," he growled. "She doesn't want to dance with you."

"Those weren't the ones," Jane whispered, as the boys retreated.

"I don't care," said Dan. "You're not going to dance with anybody until we teach you some more."

He signaled Fred, Jack, and Bob, and then guided Jane out onto a porch.

"Who did it?" Dan asked. "I'm going to show him whose sister to make passes at."

"A boy named Ned Morris," Jane told him. "He's a senior. I hope you fix him good."

Fred, Jack and Bob joined them on the porch, and Dan explained the situation.

"He's in my class," said Jack, "so I get to whip him. Right?"
Dan and Bob said that was right, but Fred disagreed.

"We spent a whole summer teaching her to be popular," he warned, "and now you want to undo it all. Nobody'll take her out if he thinks he'll have to end up by fighting us, in case he gets romantic."

"It's really our fault," Bob conceded dramatically. "We taught her how to be attractive, but we didn't teach her how to turn it off."

"I slapped him good," Jane said. "I thought that would turn it off."

"Worst thing you could do," said Fred, shaking his head. "It's our fault, all right. We'll keep a close eye on things for the rest of the night, and don't you let anybody else take you off the dance floor."

Mother was asleep when Jane and the boys returned home from the dance, but she heard them and came down in her bathrobe to help them raid the icebox. Jane wasn't upset any more, and she told Mother with considerable detail about the rush she had had.

"You're lucky to have so many brothers to help you get started," Mother said, looking proudly at the boys. "You boys have been mighty sweet to her."

"I'll say," Jane agreed excitedly. "And what do you think, Mother, tonight they're going to teach me about kissing."

"I think that's fine," said Mother, "and it's not every girl . . . They're going to teach you about what?" she shouted.

"About kissing," said Jane.

"I won't have it," Mother announced flatly. "I try to be modern. I didn't say a word when you were showing her about hand-squeezes and things like that—things most girls don't know until they're in their twenties." She raised her voice again. "But I won't have any lessons in that. The very idea!"

It took a little explaining to get across the notion that the boys were planning to teach Jane how not to be kissed. And after Mother had heard what had happened at the dance, she agreed that the instruction wasn't taking place a minute too soon.

She poured herself a glass of milk, while Fred fixed her a peanut butter sandwich, and she got plates and cut apple cake for everyone. Then, after looking around self-consciously as if she wasn't sure but what Tom would return unexpectedly from the hospital, she perched on his table.

"School's in session," she declared.

The boys asked Jane how and where it happened.

"We were dancing, and he asked me how I'd like to go out on the porch and look at the moon," she said. "I squeezed his hand, like you showed me, and said I wouldn't mind."

"No wonder you got kissed, you sap you," Dan moaned. "What did you do that for?"

"You told me to," Jane replied angrily. "Don't try to put the blame on me. You said I should try to make all of them like me. How was I supposed to know he didn't want to look at the moon?"

"Jane's right," Mother agreed. "It's not her fault."

The boys said that from now on Jane was supposed to shun parked cars and porches, and was to view with suspicion any conversation about planets, satellites, constellations, or the need for a breath of fresh air. They showed her, too, how to sit far over on her own side of the car, coming home from a date, and how to lean forward, or twist around so her back was to the door, if anyone tried to put his arm around her shoulder.

"Now if a boy kisses you anyway," said Jack, "the best squelch you can give him is to act like a dummy. The kiss doesn't affect you one way or the other. You're bored with the whole business."

"That usually gives them the idea," Bob agreed. "If it doesn't, you can wipe your lips with the back of your hand, and look as if there's something there that their best friend ought to tell them."

"Never slap them," said Fred. "A slap just makes them mad. And they still don't know whether you really object to being kissed, or whether you're playing hard-to-get."

"You boys," said Mother, disapprovingly, "seem to know a great deal about it. Where'd you find out about things like that?"

"It's information," Fred grinned, "that's handed down from father to son."

Tom died a few months later, convinced that pleurisy was the old enemy that finally had laid him low. While he was at the hospital, some of us went to see him almost every day. Sometimes he'd beg to be taken home, where he felt sure he could cure himself in a few days with his Quinine Remedy. But the doctors wouldn't allow him to be moved.

On several occasions we smuggled bottles of the Remedy into the hospital, hoping that his faith in its curative powers might make him well again. It didn't seem to affect him, one way or the other.

Tom always had been suspicious of hospitals. He had often told us his belief that doctors sometimes gave the "black bottle"—poison—to patients who didn't have plenty of money.

Toward the end, when he recognized us less frequently, he refused to take any medicines, even the Remedy.

It could be said that Tom was a man who never amounted to much. By some standards, perhaps he wasn't even a very good man. He swore a good deal, and in later years he drank more than he should have. But the day he died, twelve people wept for him.

That number may be more than par for the course.

21

ALL ALONE

THE raising of eleven children had taken a far heavier toll on our house than it had on Mother. Mother still was slim, quick, and erect, but the house was tired and sagging.

The stairs were grooved, and spokes were missing from the banisters. The furnace, never too efficient, now could be coaxed to breathe heat only into the central rooms. The floors had been scuffed beyond repair, and initials had been carved in some of the woodwork. One of the columns of the porte-cochere had begun to rot, causing the roof to angle downward like the tilt of an old rake's hat.

The year Jane was to go to college, Mother agreed with us that it was time for her to move out of the house. We thought she'd try to sell it, but she didn't like the idea of other people living in it, and she knew it wouldn't bring much money anyway. Besides needing repairs, it was built primarily for a family with ten or twelve children. People who could afford to run such a large house didn't have families that size any more.

Mother called for bids and had the house torn down. She supervised the demolition herself. If she felt any pangs as the workmen stripped off the walls and laid open the interior, she kept them to herself.

The motion study equipment, the files, the double desk she and Dad had used to perfect their original time-saving experiments went to the laboratory at Purdue. The mahogany furniture she had had since her wedding was sent to a cabinetmaker to remove the scars and stains of a generation of children and several generations of dogs and miscellaneous livestock.

Mother's finances had improved immeasurably as more consulting jobs were offered her. And now she also came into an inheritance from her family's estate. With Bob partly through college and only Jane to go, Mother could retire, if she wanted to, and relax for the rest of her life.

After years of working and scrimping, she could have fur coats, a maid to bring her breakfast in bed, even a limousine and a chauffeur, if she wanted them.

Mother didn't want them, and she had no idea of stopping work. She and Jane moved into a middle-priced apartment in Montclair. The old furniture gave a familiar appearance to Mother's new living and dining rooms—except that everything was tidy, polished and re-upholstered. She started using her best silver and china, that she had packed away years before, when Anne was starting to walk and pulling things off of tables.

A cleaning woman came twice a week, but Mother and Jane did their own cooking. With unrestricted use of her own kitchen, Mother soon became a good cook. If Jane had let Mother have her way, Jane would have been the one who had breakfast in bed. As it was, no matter how early Jane got up, her eggs and toast appeared on the table about the time she walked into the dining room.

Then Jane left for college, and Mother was alone. None of us liked the idea of that. We thought that anyone who had raised eleven youngsters always needed children in the house. Besides, it seemed only right that, after all the years she had looked out for us, we should start looking out for her.

We hadn't had a meeting of our Family Council for years, but when Anne next came to Montclair from Cleveland for a visit, we called a meeting of the Council to discuss Mother.

The Council had been one of Dad's ideas, and he had patterned it after employer-employe boards in industry. The Council had decided matters of policy, such as the size of allowances and the apportionment of house and yard work. Dad, as self-appointed chairman, had his own set of parliamentary rules, and wasn't above launching a one-man filibuster or bottling up appropriations bills in committees. But for the most part, the majority ruled.

We didn't want Mother to know about the meeting to discuss her, so we held it at Ernestine's house. It wasn't a formal session—no one presided with gavel in hand and a pitcher of ice water at his elbow, as Dad used to. But we did sit in our old positions, around Ern's dining-room table. We still looked on Anne, now a matron in her late thirties, as automatically in charge when she was home. She sat at the head of the table.

We agreed, first of all, that either Mother would move in with one of our families, or one of our families would move in with her. We felt that what had kept Mother going through the years was the goal of sending all of us through college. When that goal was achieved, there might not be any incentive to keep going, and that would mean Mother would have to make an adjustment.

[227]

We thought we'd better start preparing her, in advance, for the adjustment. We knew that many women in their sixties had had years of experience in taking things easy. They played bridge, they talked about movies and their friends, or they sat on rockers with cats on their laps.

Mother didn't know how to do any of those things, but we thought perhaps we could help her learn.

There was something else that all of us took into consideration, but hesitated to put into words. Suppose Mother should want to keep working, but as she got older the job and lecture offers should become less and less frequent. There was a rule at Purdue that faculty members had to retire when they reached seventy. That wasn't too many years in the future.

The Council appointed Ernestine to talk with Mother about moving in with one of us. If we could get Mother to do that —to forget about the idea that she might be imposing on someone—she would become interested in helping to raise another generation. Then Jane's graduation would be just another incident.

But when Ernestine put the proposition up to Mother the next day, she might as well have saved her breath.

"I can't tell you how much I appreciate it, dear," said Mother. "But I couldn't do that."

"Of course you can do it," Ernestine told her. "There's no use being stubborn."

Mother may have thought that was the pot calling the kettle black, but she realized the intentions were good, anyway.

"As long as Bob and Jane are in college," she said, "I want them to know that we—just they and I—have our own home. That's something that all of you other children had, and I think it's important for them. For me, too."

All Alone

"How about when they're out of college and married?" Ernestine asked.

"I've been thinking about that. And I don't know. Your father's mother lived with us for quite a few years after we were married. I was fond of her, and I think she was of me. But I don't think either of us really liked the situation. I don't know."

So Mother continued to live alone, except when Bob and Jane were home on vacation. And we were still worried about her.

World War II came, then. Five of the boys were in it, and overseas. Mother was older, suddenly, and sometimes she was tired.

She wrote each of the boys every day, and waited mornings for the mailman before she went into New York. She never talked about the war or how battles were going. Telegrams made her nervous; she held them up to the light before she opened them.

There were new demands on her time. We could see there wouldn't be any question about her not being busy as long as the war lasted. She was working with the War Manpower Commission. The government was using her studies on motions of the disabled, to help rehabilitate amputees. War industries wanted the latest time-saving techniques. Many of the graduates of her Motion Study Courses, which she had discontinued some years before when the engineering jobs started to come in, had important production jobs, and sought her out for consultation. Walt Disney made a training film, in technicolor, of the process chart.

She journeyed to Providence to help christen a Liberty ship named for Dad. She went to Chapel Hill for Bob's graduation. Finally the day arrived when she boarded a train to Ann Arbor, for Jane's.

[229]

That was a special occasion for Mother. She rode in a lower berth. From that time on, when the space was available, she rode in lowers.

She and Anne sat together with the spectators when Jane received her diploma. It should have been a happy occasion, because it symbolized the fulfillment of something Mother had promised herself. But when Anne thought about the sacrifices Mother had made to keep that promise, a lump settled in her throat.

Mother's youngest, handsome with her mortarboard cocked debonairly over one ear, bounded nonchalantly across the stage. She took the hand of the man who presented it—possibly giving the hand a parting squeeze—and rejoined her class.

Anne dabbed at her eyes with a handkerchief. "Jane doesn't appreciate what Mother's done for her," she thought. "None of us appreciate it. I didn't appreciate it at the time, either. I thought I did, but I didn't, really."

Jane turned around in her seat, spotted them, and waved the diploma triumphantly aloft.

"I guess Dad would be proud," Anne said, turning to Mother.

Mother didn't answer. Her eyes were closed. Her face, in repose, hadn't changed much through the years. There was the new nose, of course.

Anne waited a moment, and nudged her slightly.

"I declare, you're a great one," Anne teased. "Work a whole lifetime to send your children through college, and then go to sleep when the final great moment arrives.

Mother opened her eyes. "I wasn't asleep," she said softly. "I was saying thank you."

Both Jane and Bob were married in a year or so—all of us married young and soon had children of our own. And then the war was over and the boys began to come home. Mother seemed to shed some of the years that had piled suddenly upon her.

She thought it would be a good idea to hold a family reunion, so that all of us could see the boys and so that the three newest grandchildren could be christened together in our church in Montclair.

We converged from various parts of the country. Some of us from out of town and our families stayed at Mother's apartment, and others moved in with those who lived in or near Montclair.

Extra leaves were put back into the dining-room table, and Mother's ice box was full of baby bottles again. The good china was taken out of circulation and put on high shelves.

As Mother bathed and powdered our children, and gave them their bottles, she seemed gayer and happier than we remembered seeing her since Dad's death. When it came time to do the dishes at night, she'd take three or four of the older grandchildren back into the kitchen and they'd dry while she washed. We'd hear a lot of giggling, and know Mother was telling them stories about when we were young. Sometimes they'd sing the old songs that Mother had taught us, and we had taught them.

We whispered to each other that we couldn't understand why, since Mother seemed to enjoy our visit so much, she wouldn't move in with one of us.

On the day of the christening, we assembled at the apartment and walked the two blocks to the church. Besides Mother and the eleven of us, there were our husbands and wives and fifteen of our children, including the three babies who were to be baptized.

Two pews had been reserved for us at the front of the large, Gothic church. We walked down the center aisle as quietly as we could. But there were so many of us, and Mother knew so many people, that our entrance created a good deal of attention. Mother, ramrod straight and immensely dignified, led the delegation. We thought she looked as if she were proud of us and proud of her grandchildren. We hoped she was.

The service started. The organ music rolled out loudly, and then there was a hush and the opening prayer. Three of our boys and their wives stepped forward with their babies.

The clock turned backward for some of us.

When we were young, there was a christening in the family almost every year. And although Dad had much more experience with baptisms than the average man, they always made him nervous and irritable.

It wasn't just the christenings that he objected to—he objected to going to church for any reason. He kept saying that he was a religious man, and had nothing against churches; that he thought it was fine Mother and all of us went regularly.

But he never went himself unless there was a reason, such as a christening. And even then Mother had to prod him all the way.

Few martyrs ever looked more persecuted as they approached the stake than did Dad when, with a baby under his arm, he left the house for a christening.

"This piecemeal business of christening them one at a time is the height of inefficiency," he'd storm to Mother. "It's a by-jingoed indignation, by jingo."

"Maybe so, dear," Mother soothed him, "but I don't want to raise a houseful of heathens. One in the family is enough."

"Me a heathen?" Dad yelped. "You know I'm a religious man. But this is my final piecemeal christening. After this one, we're going to wait until the last of them is born, and then get it all over with, in one efficient ceremony."

"We can talk about that when the next one arrives," Mother smiled.

"That's what you always say. And I wind up in church with a new baby on my hands!"

Dad never had much confidence about holding babies when they were small. He was afraid he might hurt them, so he didn't grasp them firmly, and they'd wiggle until their dresses were up around their heads. When this happened, Dad would try to straighten out their clothes and get things so twisted around that Mother would have to come to the rescue.

When he stood with Mother at the front of the church, he always looked as if he wasn't quite sure whether he was holding the baby right side up. And he seemed worried that he might cause the minister to make an embarrassing blunder.

We older children would be sitting with our various Sunday school classes, in the galleries on each side of the altar, dreading what we knew we were going to do, and yet knowing that we couldn't help doing it.

We always disgraced ourselves at the christenings of our younger brothers and sisters.

As the baby squirmed in Dad's arms, while he kept peering down into the dress to make sure the head was still on top, the situation would seem more and more ludicrous to us. We'd think about how Dad had stormed beforehand, and how he was going to storm afterwards at Sunday dinner.

Then it would happen, and we would disgrace ourselves again. Suddenly, one of us would explode in a snorting giggle. You couldn't hold it back—it was embarrassing, but it was just too funny, and there wasn't anything you could do about it.

Another one of us, sitting with another class and vowing that this time he could control himself, would hear the snort, and he would explode too. Finally, all of us would be giggling, and people down in the congregation would crane their necks to see what was causing the disturbance.

Since Dad only went to church for the christening of his own children, he comforted himself with the thought that a few jackasses in the balcony always giggled whenever a child was baptized. Although this belief was completely erroneous, we did our best not to dispel it.

"Worst-mannered congregation I ever saw," he'd complain afterwards. "They seem to think a christening is like a vaude- . ville show."

Bob's baby was a wiggler. As Bob and his wife and the two other couples stood in front of the minister, the dress of Bob's daughter started to slide over her head. With considerable concern, Bob looked down. Just for a minute, it was Dad all over again. Just for a minute, the older ones who were sitting with Mother were little children again, up in the galleries with their Sunday school classes.

Ernestine had a horrible thought. Suppose she should suddenly start to giggle? It was bad enough when a child did that. But suppose an adult, herself the mother of two children, should do it? It was out of the question, of course. Adults could control themselves. They simply didn't make scenes like that.

Bob's daughter wiggled some more, and Bob looked down again to find her head.

Ernestine snorted. She put her hand over her mouth, but the giggle came out through her nose. You could hear it all all over the church.

Ernestine's husband and children looked at her with amazement. Mother hunched her shoulders instinctively, and kept her eyes straight ahead, as if Ernestine were someone else's daughter who had got into our group by mistake.

Ernestine tried biting her lips, but it was no use. She sat there and giggled. So did the rest of us, in a series of moist explosions. So, although she still denies it, did Mother. There are witnesses to prove it.

So did the congregation and so did the minister—he had been at the church for years, and recalled the old days. Fortunately the christening service hadn't quite started; he stopped everything and laughed until he had to dig under his vestments to get a handkerchief.

Finally there was quiet again, and the three babies were baptized. The minister climbed back into the pulpit, and looked down at us. We weren't too happy about the way we had behaved.

"I don't know as I'd want to go through it all over again and have the eleven of you up in the balcony every Sunday," he began. "I'm not as young as I used to be. But it's good to have you here on a visit. It's good to see you together again. Mighty good!"

We glanced at Mother to see how she was taking it, and for the first time we knew for certain why she lived alone. We knew that, glad as she was to have us home, she lived alone because she liked it.

For Mother was nodding agreement. She didn't want to go through with it all over again, either. One generation was enough.

Mother looked as if the minister had taken the words right out of her mouth.

All Alone

Mother still lives in the same apartment. She retired from Purdue when she reached seventy, but she is busier than ever today.

Not long ago, the American Society of Mechanical Engineers and the American Management Association awarded to her, and to Dad posthumously, the Gantt medal for "pioneer work in management and the development of the principles and techniques of motion study." And the American Women's Association named her Woman of the Year.

Even those of us on the West Coast see her four or five times a year, because she has a good many lectures there. Those who live in or near Montclair drop by the apartment fairly often after dinner when she's home, and to sort and forward her mail when she's away.

Before she leaves town on business trips, Mother makes out an itinerary listing the hotels and the persons' houses where she will be stopping. At the bottom of the itinerary, it says:

"I know you'll call me, if you need me."